International Liquidity Issues

International Liquidity Issues

Thomas D. Willett

American Enterprise Institute for Public Policy Research
Washington, D.C.

Thomas D. Willett, an AEI adjunct scholar and Horton Professor of Economics at Claremont Graduate School and Claremont Men's College, has served as deputy assistant secretary of the treasury for international research.

Library of Congress Cataloging in Publication Data

Willett, Thomas D
    International liquidity issues.

    (AEI studies ; 283)
    Bibliography: p.
    1. International liquidity. I. American Enterprise Institute for Public Policy Research. II. United States. Congress. Joint Economic Committee. Special Study on Economic Change. III. Title. IV. Series: American Enterprise Institute for Public Policy Research. AEI studies ; 283.
HG3893.W54   332.4'5   80–18074
ISBN 0–8447–3388–1

AEI Studies 283

Printed in the United States of America

Contents

Acknowledgments

In preparing this study I have benefited from discussions with economists and practitioners in Washington and the academic community too numerous to list. I should like, however, especially to thank Peter Clark, Andrew Crockett, Jacob Dreyer, Gottfried Haberler, Leroy Laney, John Mullen, Carter Murphy, Robert Sammons, and Edward Tower for helpful comments on earlier drafts of this manuscript, without implying that they necessarily agree with all of the conclusions drawn. I am also grateful to Lisa Skoog, of AEI's publications staff, who edited this volume.

International Liquidity Issues

1

Introduction

Although the international monetary system underwent major reform during the 1970s, this did not quiet controversy about international monetary problems. Considerable concern has been expressed that deficiencies in the mechanism for the provision and control of international liquidity may have been major causes of worldwide inflation and currency instability, and that our new international monetary system based on more flexible exchange rates does not adequately deal with these problems.

There have always been differences of judgment whether international reserves were growing too rapidly or too slowly and about what forms international reserve holdings should take. Should more reliance be placed on gold, on the dollar, on some combination of major currencies, or on an international paper unit? Such was the focus of the international liquidity controversies of the 1960s. These controversies were quite sufficient to generate a huge literature by professional economists and international monetary experts on international liquidity issues and to stimulate a major series of international political negotiations that culminated in the historic agreements creating a new type of official international money, the special drawing rights (SDRs) administered through the International Monetary Fund.

Far from resolving international liquidity disputes, however, the creation of the SDR was soon followed by a series of international financial developments that have necessitated a complete rethinking of the nature of international liquidity issues and how we should analyze them.

The old sources of controversy have not disappeared, although their exact nature and importance have been substantially modified in many instances, and many new international liquidity questions have been generated as well. The rapid growth of international financial markets and the substantial increase in the extent to which national governments both supply funds to and borrow funds from these markets has tended to blur the traditional distinctions between private and official international liquidity, and has raised serious questions about the control of international liquidity growth. The rapid growth of the Eurocurrency markets has similarly caused many to question the extent to which national monetary authorities can control their domestic financial conditions, and has further fueled fears that at present our international financial system is an engine for world inflation.

The potential magnitude of such concerns about liquidity expansion is illustrated by two explosions of official international liquidity: the first, generated by the massive U.S. balance-of-payments deficits and accompanying breakdown of the Bretton Woods exchange-rate arrangements in the early 1970s; and the second, accompanying the huge increases in oil prices in 1973 and 1974 with the resulting enormous balance-of-payments surpluses for OPEC and the corresponding deficits for most oil-importing countries. Over the 1970–1972 period international reserves created by the official intervention of surplus countries grew by roughly as much as they had in the whole preceding part of the postwar period. The high rates of inflation throughout the world that were temporarily associated with these developments have strongly reinforced fears that our current international financial arrangements are dangerously deficient.

At the same time that the potential effects of international liquidity issues on the operation of the world economy have reached enormous proportions, our ability to analyze the implications of changes in the levels of recorded international reserves has been affected by greatly increased uncertainties. The growth of international capital mobility could be expected to increase greatly official demands for international liquidity to offset the greater potential size of disturbances to countries' balance-of-payments positions. On the other hand, government measures to attract internationally mobile capital and direct government borrowings in private financial markets have been important in supplementing countries' owned reserves. The net effects of these factors are difficult to predict and are likely to vary greatly from one country to another.[1]

---

[1] For an interesting critique of the failure to consider private capital flows in much of the literature on international reserves, and for a presentation of the "new" efficient-markets view of private capital flows as a substitute for official reserve flows, see K. L. Mahar and M. G. Porter, "International Reserves and Capital Mobility," in Robert

Likewise, it is difficult to assess the effects of changing positions of gold on the effective magnitude of international liquidity. On the one hand, gold has been officially demonetized in many respects. On the other hand, gold can still be sold to supplement countries' holdings of foreign exchange and can be, and has been, used as collateral for official loans. Over the past year, its market price has fluctuated between roughly six and eight times its pre-1971 official price. Again, the net effects are difficult to assess.

Of perhaps even greater importance is the fact that we need to rethink substantially the role of various aspects of the traditional international liquidity issues in our new international monetary system based on considerable flexibility of exchange rates for the major industrial countries. The major purpose of this study is to aid in this process of rethinking by discussing how we should analyze international liquidity issues in a new international monetary environment. It is not by any means the first such effort, nor will it be the last. It is hoped, however, that the following sections will offer a helpful framework for analyzing current and likely future international liquidity issues over the coming decade.

This study is divided into two major parts. The first and longer is an analytic history of major international liquidity concepts and issues. It attempts to merge a review of the evolution of major international liquidity developments and policy issues with presentations of major elements of international liquidity theory. A major aspect of this part of the study is an evaluation of the similarities and differences between the manner in which the behavior of national monetary aggregates can be used to control the macroeconomic performance of domestic economies and the way that international reserve aggregates can be used to control the operation of the world economy. Such analogies have often played a prominent role in the development of views that our current international liquidity mechanism may be dangerously inadequate and in proposals for reform. More detailed research indicates, however, that there may be many differences between the effects on economic behavior of changes in monetary aggregates and changes in international reserve aggregates.

In general the following analysis suggests that as the international monetary system has evolved from a gold standard to the Bretton Woods system based on adjustable pegged exchange rates

Z. Aliber, ed., *The Political Economy of Monetary Reform* (Montclair, N.J.: Allanheld, Osmun and Co., 1977), pp. 205–19. On the limitations of using monetary policy to attract private capital flows, see Thomas D. Willett, "Official versus Market Financing of International Deficits," *Kyklos*, fasc. 3 (1968), pp. 514–24, and Thomas D. Willett and Francesco Forte, "Interest-Rate Policy and External Balance," *Quarterly Journal of Economics*, vol. 83, no. 2 (May 1969), pp. 242–62.

and reserve currencies, and from that to the current system based on managed flexibility of exchange rates and widespread official use of private international financial markets, there has been a progressive weakening of the usefulness of reserve aggregates as a control mechanism for the operation of the world economy. Indeed, in recent years attempts to restrict the growth of international reserve aggregates to keep them in line with historical relationships between such totals and world trade and payments could have been disastrous. Trade warfare and a severe worsening of the worldwide recession of 1974–1975 might have resulted.

My analysis is relatively complacent in the sense that it finds that the more alarmist views of severe dangers from the operation of current mechanisms are generally based on seriously oversimplified views. For example, figures showing the Eurodollar markets now several times larger than the domestic supply of dollars do not mean that the U.S. monetary authorities have lost control over U.S. monetary conditions, as is sometimes implied. The most serious case in which the operation of the international monetary system has itself been a major stimulant to world inflation involved the breakdown of the Bretton Woods system. Disaggregate research suggests, however, that this impact, while certainly to be deplored, was much less than much popular discussion has assumed. Furthermore, the subsequent adoption of floating exchange rates offers much greater protection against a recurrence of such excessive international liquidity creation. In short, although our current international liquidity arrangements do not conform to a tidy blueprint for international monetary control, they are not nearly as dangerously inadequate as many have feared. Our current loose decentralized system of international liquidity creation has more built-in stabilizing mechanisms than many have recognized.

This more optimistic or complacent view does not, however, imply that our current international financial arrangements are perfect. What it does imply is that international liquidity questions and controls can best be analyzed in connection with direct analysis of the operation of the balance-of-payments and exchange-rate adjustment process and its international surveillance and control, rather than primarily from the standpoint of the behavior of international liquidity aggregates.[2]

---

[2] In recent years, a number of international monetary experts have reached a similar conclusion. See, for example, Andrew D. Crockett, "Control over International Reserves," *IMF Staff Papers*, vol. 25, no. 1 (Washington, D.C.: International Monetary Fund, 1978), pp. 1–24; Gottfried Haberler, "How Important Is Control over Interna-

The second part of this study is forward looking. It considers some of the major international liquidity issues that we are likely to face over the coming decade and analyzes some of the major types of proposals suggested for dealing with these issues. The issues include the future role of the SDR, the control of international liquidity, and the so-called dollar overhang and instability problems caused by the existence of multiple reserve assets. Although the justification for the perspective of analysis adopted in chapter 3 is developed in detail in chapter 2, the study is designed so that readers interested only in the analysis of current policy issues may turn directly to chapter 3.

---

tional Reserves?" in Robert Mundell and Jacques J. Polak, eds., *The New International Monetary System* (New York: Columbia University Press, 1977), pp. 111–32; Peter B. Kenen, "Techniques to Control International Reserves," in ibid., pp. 202–22; Robert Solomon, "Techniques to Control International Reserves," in ibid., pp. 185–201; Robert Slighton, "International Liquidity Issues under Flexible Exchange Rates," in Jacob Dreyer, Gottfried Haberler, and Thomas D. Willett, eds., *Exchange-Rate Flexibility* (Washington, D.C.: American Enterprise Institute, 1978), pp. 229–40; and my own earlier analysis, Thomas D. Willett, *Floating Exchange Rates and International Monetary Reform* (Washington, D.C.: American Enterprise Institute, 1977).

2

An Analytic History of International Liquidity Concepts and Developments

Discussions of international liquidity issues frequently focus on international reserves as a means of regulating the operation of the world economy. There was considerable professional concern with international reserve issues during the 1960s, culminating in the creation of the SDR. In recent years widespread concern with such questions has increased still further, largely as the result of the resurgence of interest in what is often called global or international monetarism. This view assumes that control over the rate of growth in international reserves will influence macroeconomic development in the world economy in much the same way that variations in the rate of growth of an individual country's money stock will influence that country's macroeconomic performance. This view has been expressed by several leading academic economists and by many people of practical affairs, such as bankers, businessmen, journalists, and financial officials.[1]

In part, this focus reflects the general resurgence of attention paid to monetary factors in reaction to the long period of post-Keynes-

---

[1] See, for example, the discussions and references to the literature in Richard J. Sweeney and Thomas D. Willett, "Eurodollars, Petrodollars, and Problems of World Liquidity and Inflation," in Karl Brunner and Allan H. Meltzer, eds., *Stabilization of the Domestic and International Economy*, vol. 5 of the Carnegie-Rochester Conference Series on Public Policy, a Supplementary Series to the *Journal of Monetary Economics* (1977), pp. 277–310; Marina Whitman, "Global Monetarism and the Monetary Approach to the Balance of Payments," *Brookings Papers on Economic Activity*, no. 3 (Washington, D.C.: Brookings Institution, 1975), pp. 491–555; John Williamson, "International Liquidity: A Survey," *Economic Journal*, vol. 83, no. 331 (September 1973), pp. 685–764; and Thomas D. Willett, *Floating Exchange Rates and International Monetary Reform* (Washington, D.C.: American Enterprise Institute, 1977), chap. 4. These four authors do not themselves adopt an international monetarism approach. A recent example of this view is given in the following statement by H. Johannes Witteveen, former managing director of the In-

ian deemphasis of such considerations. The current popularity of this view no doubt also received considerable stimulus from the huge explosion in international liquidity in the early 1970s, which was accompanied by rapid monetary expansion in Europe and subsequent acceleration in the rate of inflation—facts that are in accord with the international monetarist view. Nor can there be any doubt that there is a significant element of truth in the international monetarist interpretation of this episode.

As will be argued below, however, there are strong reasons to believe that the rapid expansion of monetary growth in the industrial countries in the early 1970s was due to more than just the explosion of international liquidity during that period. Nor are the effects of given increases in international reserves on the world economy likely to be independent of the causes of these increases, their distribution among countries, and the type of international monetary regime in operation. This conclusion is the basic theme for this chapter. Although the international monetarist views point to some important elements that should not be overlooked, they cannot safely be taken in their strong forms as an all-purpose guide to international liquidity relationships.

This strong view would perhaps best be termed *international reserve monetarism*. Arguments that there is not a tremendously strong linkage between international reserves and world inflation need not imply that there is not a strong relationship between global monetary aggregates and world inflation. In other words, criticism of international reserve monetarism as a guide to international liquidity policy need not rest on beliefs that monetary considerations are minor or that there is little use in looking at relationships between global monetary aggregates and world inflation. Rather, the critique of international reserve monetarism offered here rests on the argument that the relationships between national governments' economic behavior and their international reserve holdings are much more complex than those between the injection of greater money balances into the private economy and the resulting spending decisions of private economic agents.[2] Not only is there much more scope for the law of large numbers to even out random factors in the case of private economic

ternational Monetary Fund: "But it seems to me that just as in a domestic system, one can hardly control inflation without having some control of the money creation by the banking system, so, too, one must control world liquidity in order to influence world inflation." [H. Johannes Witteveen, "A Conversation with Mr. Witteveen," *Finance and Development*, vol. 15, no. 3 (September 1978), p. 8.]

[2] For analysis of differences between the world demand for international reserves and the demand for money in individual economies, see Pekka Ahtiala, "Monetary Policy

decisions, but the importance of imbalances between national governments' demand and supply of international reserves is likely to be a less important motivator of their economic behavior over a wide range than would be comparable imbalances between the demand and supply of money for private economic agents. The costs of correcting imbalances between the demand and supply of international reserves will often be much greater relative to the costs of holding nonoptimal reserve positions than is typically the case with respect to the demand and supply of national currencies.

These points may be illustrated by considering a stylized view of the evolution of the international monetary system and national macroeconomic policy making. As we shall see, the thrust of the history of this century has been away from the conditions under which the strong international reserve monetarist view would be expected to have its highest explanatory power.

The Gold Standard Rules of the Game

We begin this review with an idealized version of the liberal gold standard that operated among many of the major industrial countries from the latter part of the nineteenth century until 1913. While the actual operation of this system was much more complex in practice, the textbook version of the operation of the idealized gold standard presents the world of international monetarism at its strongest.[3]

Under this idealized system, countries are committed to liberal trade policies, fixed exchange rates, and long-run equilibrium in the balance of payments. The "rules of the game" are that surpluses and deficits in the balance of payments should be allowed to have their full impact on national money supplies. If a country is gaining re-

---

in National and International Economics," in *International Reserves: Needs and Availability* (Washington, D.C.: International Monetary Fund, 1970); Richard N. Cooper, "International Liquidity and Balance of Payments Adjustment," in ibid., pp. 125–45; Jacques J. Polak, "Money: National and International," in ibid., pp. 510–20; Andrew D. Crockett, "Control over International Reserves," *IMF Staff Papers*, vol. 25, no. 1 (Washington, D.C.: International Monetary Fund, 1978), pp. 1–24; Egon Sohmen, "International Liquidity Issues: Discussion," in Jacob Dreyer, Gottfried Haberler, and Thomas D. Willett, eds., *Exchange-Rate Flexibility* (Washington, D.C.: American Enterprise Institute, 1978), pp. 255–63; Sweeney and Willett, "Eurodollars, Petrodollars, and World Liquidity," pp. 277–310; Willett, *Floating Exchange Rates*, chap. 4; and Williamson, "International Liquidity," pp. 685–764.

[3] For analysis of the actual operation of the gold standard during the nineteenth and twentieth centuries, see A. I. Bloomfield, *Monetary Policy under the International Gold*

serves because of a balance-of-payments surplus, then its money supply must be allowed to expand. If it is running a balance-of-payments deficit and losing reserves, then its money supply should be allowed to contract. These effects would occur automatically as long as the monetary authorities refrained from offsetting the effects of reserve flows on the monetary base—that is, if they did not sterilize the effects of these reserve inflows and outflows.

In this idealized world, international obligations always took precedence over domestic economic objectives and international reserve flows were the major determinant of countries' macroeconomic policies. This self-regulating mechanism assured long-run equilibrium in a country's balance of payments by placing inflationary pressures on surplus countries and deflationary pressures on deficit countries. Furthermore, in the strong form of this system, under which there was a fixed average ratio between gold holdings and national money supplies, variations in gold supply would determine the rate of increase or decrease of the world price level.[4] Adjustments to reserve flows would assure that the price-level effects of new gold discoveries would be spread throughout the system.

In versions of the gold standard in which gold was used as an international reserve for transactions among governments but could not be obtained on demand by private citizens in exchange for national currency, there was no natural limit to the ratio between gold stocks and national money supplies. When there were no required ratios of gold backing for the national money supply, then national policy decisions, as well as variations in gold supply, could influence the world price level.

Although the link between gold supply and the world price level could be broken in this manner, there would still be a strong systematic relationship between reserve changes and changes in the rate of expansion of a country's money supply. As long as countries continued to follow the "rules of the game," those countries with balance-of-payments surpluses would have to allow their national money supplies to expand more rapidly than otherwise, while for deficit

Standard: 1880–1914 (New York: Federal Reserve Board, 1959); John Dutton, "Effective Protection, Taxes on Foreign Investment, and the Operation of the Gold Standard" (Ph.D. diss., Duke University, 1978), chap. 3; D. N. McCloskey and J. R. Zecher, "How the Gold Standard Worked, 1880–1913," in J. A. Frenkel and H. G. Johnson, eds., *The Monetary Approach to the Balance of Payments* (London: Allen and Unwin, 1976); Thomas D. Willett, "Official versus Market Financing of International Deficits," *Kyklos*, fasc. 3 (1968), pp. 514–24; Leland B. Yeager, *International Monetary Relations* (New York: Harper and Row, 1976), chap. 15; and references cited in these works.
[4] Of course, the level of output and the velocity of money would also affect the level of prices through the famous quantity theory equation $MV = PT$.

countries just the reverse would occur. Countries' rates of monetary expansion no longer would be constrained directly by the gold supply, but rather by the average rate of monetary expansion in the system as a whole. Thus the gold standard system never offered insurance against inflation per se, only against inflation consistently greater than the average for other countries.[5] The gold standard did not necessarily protect countries from "imported inflation," although it did strongly limit the extent to which a single (nongold-producing) country could export domestic inflationary pressures to others.

The Rise of Concern with Domestic Macroeconomic Conditions

Although such a system looked very attractive because it automatically corrected international payments imbalances, this success was achieved at the cost of subjecting domestic monetary conditions to the dictates of the balance of payments. Historical research shows that the major countries were never willing to play entirely by the rules of the game, and for sound reasons. When wages and prices were not highly flexible downwards, deflationary pressures in deficit countries would result not just in falling prices, but also in falling output and rising unemployment.

Nor would full wage and price flexibility eliminate all of the costs of subjecting the internal economy to the dictates of the balance of payments. Price stability was itself an important objective; much of the early debate over fixed versus flexible exchange rates was phrased in terms of the relative importance of pursuing the stability of internal or external prices. Both Irving Fisher and John Maynard Keynes were leading advocates of the view that internal price stability was of the greater importance.[6]

As concern with unemployment grew and knowledge of the

---

[5] Rates of inflation can vary among sectors of an economy, of course. In Japan, for example, export prices remained virtually constant during the 1960s, despite a considerable increase in the overall price level, because of high productivity growth in the export sectors. Thus, even under a fixed-rate system there can be differences in the behavior of a country's overall price indexes, but in the long run the price-structure will be forced to conform to global price developments. For further discussion, and for references to the literature on this subject, see Lawrence H. Officer, "The Purchasing Power Parity Theory of Exchange Rates: A Review Article," *IMF Staff Papers*, vol. 23, no. 1 (Washington, D.C.: International Monetary Fund, 1976), pp. 1–60, and Sweeney and Willett, "Eurodollars, Petrodollars, and Liquidity," pp. 277–310.

[6] For references to these discussions, see Willett, *Floating Exchange Rates*, and Marie Thursby and Thomas D. Willett, "The Effects of Flexible Exchange Rates on International Trade and Investment," mimeographed (Claremont, Calif.: Claremont Graduate School, 1980), forthcoming in Richard J. Sweeney and Thomas D. Willett, eds., *Studies on Exchange Rate Flexibility* (Washington, D.C.: American Enterprise Institute).

effects of macroeconomic policies on domestic economic conditions expanded, governments came under increasing pressure to resolve conflicts between the dictates of balance-of-payments equilibrium and domestic economic objectives in favor of the latter. It was still recognized that balance-of-payments equilibrium was necessary in the long run, but with ample international reserves, countries could finance payments deficits for a considerable period of time. Thus countries would often continue to follow expansionary monetary and fiscal policies in the short run even if they were running a balance-of-payments deficit. Likewise, surplus countries concerned with holding down inflation would have to offset—that is, sterilize—at least part of the effects of reserve inflows on the rate of domestic monetary expansion.

As adjusting domestic macroeconomic policies to the dictates of the balance of payments increasingly became perceived as being very costly, the demands for ample supplies of international reserves increased accordingly. Indeed, until this decade, virtually all of the international discussions of international liquidity were prompted by concerns that available supplies were not adequate for smooth functioning of the international monetary system.[7]

In the newer versions of the pegged exchange-rate systems, considerable "elasticity" was introduced into the international liquidity mechanism, both in terms of the supply of international liquidity and in the relationships between international reserve flows and countries' macroeconomic policies. In terms of the elasticity of the supply of international reserves, countries began to economize on gold (and created reserves in the process) by holding key foreign currencies, initially largely in pounds sterling, as a part of their international reserves. Thus the gold standard evolved into a gold-exchange standard.

Likewise, the international monetary system became less automatic. The question of how international adjustment responsibilities would be divided began to emerge as a central aspect of international monetary conflict. Once they recognized that balance-of-payments adjustment is costly, national governments wanted policies which would reduce their own need to make such adjustments. Each government would prefer another to bear the necessary costs of adjusting to the mutual payments imbalances.

Under the rules of the game of the gold standard, such adjust-

---

[7] On this point, see Gottfried Haberler, "How Important Is Control over International Reserves?" in Robert Mundell and Jacques J. Polak, eds., *The New International Monetary System* (New York: Columbia University Press, 1977), pp. 111–32, and Robert Solomon, "Techniques to Control International Reserves," ibid., pp. 185–201.

ment responsibilities were automatically determined, at least in theory. The problem of "who should adjust" did not arise. It became generally recognized, however, that under modern conditions such rules were not workable. Immediate adjustments of macroeconomic policies to achieve payments equilibrium were viewed as being much too costly for most countries.

Often payments imbalances were caused by temporary or cyclical factors that would reverse themselves in a few months or a few years. International reserve flows and sterilization policies would let countries wait out these temporary imbalances without sacrificing domestic economic objectives. Furthermore, even when adjustments were required, it was widely believed that such adjustments would be less costly if they could be spread out over a longer period of time. Thus prolonged payments deficits became socially acceptable and what has been called "the international disequilibrium system" emerged.[8]

The International Disequilibrium System and the Allocation of Adjustment Pressures

One of the major difficulties with this system was that there was no systematic guidance for when countries should adjust. It was generally accepted that there were good and valid reasons for not adjusting immediately, but there was no general agreement on when adjustment should begin. There is a strong presumption that while the automaticity of the gold standard "rules of the game" would have imposed high social costs through excessively rapid adjustment, systems which emerged later generated powerful incentives for each country to adjust less promptly than would have been collectively optimal.

There was a normal tendency to engage in excessive wishful thinking that a natural turnaround in the balance of payments was just around the corner, and hence policy actions could be avoided. Furthermore, the longer one waited, the greater was the likelihood that the other parties to mutual payments imbalances would themselves finally take adjustment actions, alleviating, or at least reducing, the need for the home country to do so. This expected possibility of throwing a greater share of the adjustment costs off onto others presents a classic case of splits between private and social interests that

---

[8] See Robert Mundell, "The International Disequilibrium System," *Kyklos*, fasc. 3 (1961), pp. 154–72.

can lead the collection of optimal individual decisions into inefficient social outcomes.[9]

In a different international economic environment the same type of problem existed during the Great Depression of the 1930s, when country after country tried to stimulate domestic employment through devaluations and protectionist trade policies. While such policies could make sense from the standpoint of the welfare of an individual country, trade surpluses could not be run by all countries. The net result of such attempts was a crippling of world trade that ended up by reducing, rather than increasing, employment for most countries.

Since the days of Adam Smith's discussion of the "invisible hand," economists have tended to advocate the adoption of institutional mechanisms that minimize the divergencies between the incentives for individual self-interest and the behavioral requirements for socially desirable outcomes. In effect, the international adjustment process has substantial elements of being a public good, and individual countries can have an incentive to seek a free ride. The greater the cost of providing the public good, the adjustment of payments disequilibrium, the more we would expect that public good to be underprovided in the absence of some formal or informal collective agreement.

The gold standard "rules of the game" provided such a type of collective agreement, at least in theory, but it imposed what were perceived to be excessive social costs. The "ideal" adjustment system under fixed exchange rates would have provided a desirable set of standards for deciding when countries should adjust. Unfortunately, however, there was not the technical basis for objectively and unambiguously determining such a set of standards, nor could we have been assured of political acceptance of such criteria even if they had been devised. The actual allocation of adjustment actions was left de facto to the combination of informal pressures of participants in a conflict situation, the parameters of which were conditioned by the amount of international liquidity in the system.

The greater the stock of international liquidity, the more prolonged were the payments imbalances that could be run by deficit countries, and the greater were the pressures for adjustment by sur-

---

[9] This is one of the major topics emphasized in the literature on public choice theory. For a general survey of this literature, see Dennis C. Mueller, *Public Choice* (Cambridge, England: Cambridge University Press, 1979). On applications to international economic relations, see Thomas D. Willett, "Some Aspects of the Public Choice Approach to International Economic Relations" (Paper presented at the European University Institute Conference on New Economic Approaches to the Study of International Integration, Florence, Italy, May 31-June 2, 1979), forthcoming in the conference volume to be edited by Pierre Salmon.

plus countries, either because of the limited ability to sterilize the effects of monetary inflows or because of the mounting economic distortions generated by the payments imbalances themselves. It was frequently argued that too much of the burden of adjustment tended to be placed on deficit countries because there was a limit to the size and duration of the deficits they could run, set by the availability of international liquidity. Surplus countries felt pressures to adjust as well, however. In the first place, for many smaller economies with underdeveloped domestic capital markets, monetary authorities had only limited ability to offset the domestic financial effects of balance-of-payments surpluses. And even for larger economies with better developed domestic financial markets, continued sterilization of large balance-of-payments surpluses could result in increasing dislocations in the allocation of credit across sectors, with expansion in domestic sectors having to be held down to offset the growth of liquidity accruing to the international sectors.

Furthermore, large and growing balance-of-payments surpluses were increasingly recognized as involving a less than optimal allocation of the nation's resources. Many governments found it most comfortable to run moderate balance-of-payments surpluses. This was greeted with much more support by exporters than opposition by consumers. Surpluses could become too large, however, and induce pressures to adjust.

Thus there were pressures on both surplus and deficit countries to adjust, but they were far from automatic. In this context, the rate of expansion of international liquidity became a major determinant of the distribution of adjustment pressures between surplus and deficit countries. Under fixed exchange rates, a more rapid expansion of international liquidity would tend to raise the world price level by lessening the need for deflationary pressures in deficit countries and consequently placing greater pressures on surplus countries to take on more of the burden of adjusting to mutual imbalances.

In this system the international reserve monetarist view of the relationships between changes in international reserves and world inflation continued to have a good deal of validity, although the empirical relationships were likely to be loose. There were few well-defined limits at which surplus or even deficit countries would begin to adjust. Thus, while the direction of effects was clear, the timing and magnitude of these effects could be quite variable.

International Liquidity and the Adjustable Peg System

The linkages between changes in international reserves and macroeconomic policies are further weakened when the assumptions of free-trade policies and fixed exchange rates are dropped. With exchange rates fixed, the alternatives for correcting a balance-of-payments deficit are less expansionary domestic macroeconomic policies or the imposition of import barriers and controls. Given increased perceptions of downward wage and price inflexibilities and concerns about avoiding unemployment, governments that found themselves running low on international reserves often imposed trade barriers and controls rather than deflate their economies. To a lesser extent, surplus countries would sometimes respond with trade liberalization. Thus, even when the distribution of adjustment was known, the resulting effects on the world economy would depend on the adjustment instruments chosen.

The same, of course, holds with respect to the use of exchange-rate adjustments. The designers of our postwar international monetary system were skeptical of freely floating exchange rates, associating them with the economic chaos of the 1930s.[10] They wished equally to avoid the use of trade barriers to adjust the balance of payments, however, and felt that the discipline of a new gold standard would often require excessive deflationary policies and high unemployment in deficit countries. The preferred solution of Lord Keynes, the chief British negotiator at Bretton Woods, was an ample supply of international liquidity so that balance-of-payments adjustment actions would be a last resort. When payments imbalances failed to cancel out over a long period of time and adjustment actions were clearly required, Keynes and most of the Bretton Woods negotiators preferred to use exchange-rate adjustments rather than deflationary policies in deficit countries and inflationary policies in surplus countries.

Given his desire to avoid correcting balance-of-payments deficits through unemployment in deficit countries, Keynes recognized that there was a trade-off between the availability of international liquidity and the frequency with which exchange rates would need to be adjusted. Keynes himself preferred relatively greater reliance on abundant international liquidity and less reliance on exchange-rate adjustments. However, it became clear that the U.S. Congress would not go along with Keynes's imaginative proposals for what was, in effect, a true international central bank, empowered to create international money. Indeed, the Congress would be willing to provide only quite limited funds for an international organization (the International Monetary Fund) to lend to deficit countries. Keynes recognized that there would be a need for a much greater amount of exchange-rate adjustment than he had originally envisioned.

---

[10] On the establishment of the postwar international monetary system, see Willett, *Floating Exchange Rates*, chap. 1, and the references cited there.

He likewise recognized the need for international provisions for adjustment pressures that would operate more directly than through the availability of international liquidity. As a part of his proposal for an international central bank, Keynes had advocated a symmetrical graduated set of financial penalties to be placed on both surplus and deficit countries as their cumulative imbalances increased. With the death of his central bank proposal, this idea appears to have been dropped as well. The problem was officially recognized, but the solution adopted proved to be quite inadequate in practice. The scarce currency clause provided that trade discrimination could be sanctioned against a country in excessive surplus, and that the offending member could even be expelled from the International Monetary Fund. This proved to be much too blunt an instrument for practical use, however, and it was never invoked.

Likewise, although most of the negotiators at Bretton Woods recognized that the limited provisions for international liquidity adopted meant that greater use of exchange-rate adjustments would be required for efficient operation of the international monetary system, the provisions made for using exchange rates did not work well in practice. Extrapolating from the period between the two world wars, many of the Bretton Woods negotiators feared that the major problem of the postwar period would be to hold in check governments' propensities to engage in too many exchange-rate adjustments. Instead, however, the problem turned out to be that exchange-rate adjustments were used too infrequently.

Official prestige became associated with maintaining constant exchange rates, and the economic shocks and income redistribution that would accompany occasional large exchange-rate adjustments were viewed by governments in both surplus and deficit countries as being likely to generate more political costs than benefits.[11] These problems were exacerbated by the gradual decline in capital controls and accompanying increases in the quantities of speculative and precautionary movements of funds in the anticipation of possible exchange-rate adjustments. Although for most industrial countries the use of exchange-rate adjustments offered an option that reduced the economic cost of balance-of-payments adjustment, the environment of the Bretton Woods system generated large disincentives to the use of this instrument. In practice, the provision for exchange-rate adjustments did little to reduce the problem of deciding who would adjust to mutual payments imbalances.

Although attempts were made to develop a code for determining adjustment responsibilities through the work of the Working Party

---

[11] See, for example, the discussion in J. Carter Murphy, *The International Monetary System* (Washington, D.C.: American Enterprise Institute, 1979).

Three of the Organization for Economic Cooperation and Development (OECD), the accomplishments were quite modest. There was general agreement with the principle that both surplus and deficit countries should participate in the adjustment to mutual imbalances. This may have made surplus countries somewhat susceptible to informal pressures from others to adjust, but in practice disputes over who should adjust continued unabated. Views of the exchange-rate system were that it was so fragile that the role of exchange-rate adjustments could not even be mentioned during the adjustment responsibility discussions of the mid-1960s.

Again, much of the debate over the operation of the adjustment mechanism fell back to the question of the provision of international liquidity. Representatives of deficit countries tended to view the growth of international liquidity as too slow; they advanced new provisions for expanding international liquidity. Surplus countries, on the other hand, viewed the prospect of greater international liquidity provisions largely as a way for deficit countries to export inflationary pressures. Thus, surplus countries tended to oppose efforts to expand the supply of international liquidity. Of course, not all countries stayed perpetually in a surplus or deficit status, and views on aggregate international liquidity policies were not completely determined by a country's current balance-of-payments position, but these tendencies did carry a great deal of explanatory power.

Thus, again, we see views of international liquidity issues as being largely conditioned by views of the operation of the adjustment process; changes in international liquidity were considered an indirect method through which to influence the operation of the adjustment process when more direct methods of control were not in operation.

Determining Reserve Adequacy

What about the role of objective economic studies in determining how much international liquidity was really needed? Could not such technical analysis have been substituted for the political bickering of surplus and deficit countries?

There has been a great deal of very useful technical, theoretical, and empirical work on international liquidity.[12] Unfortunately, how-

---

[12] Useful reviews of this literature have been presented by Benjamin J. Cohen, "International Reserves and Liquidity," in Peter B. Kenen, ed., International Trade and Finance (Cambridge, England: Cambridge University Press, 1975); Herbert G. Grubel, "The Demand for International Reserves: A Critical Review of the Literature," Journal of Economic Literature, vol. 9, no. 4 (December 1971), pp. 1148–66; F. Steb. Hipple, The Disturbances Approach to the Demand for International Reserves, Princeton Studies in International Finance, no. 35 (Princeton, N.J.: International Finance Section, Princeton University, 1974); and Williamson, "International Liquidity," pp. 685–764.

ever, this research could not resolve these types of disputes. We do know a great deal about empirical regularities in countries' demands for international reserves.[13] We know that, as the size and variability of a country's international payments grow, it will tend to want to hold great international reserves. Thus, we know that to maintain a given degree of reserve ease, the stock of international reserves should increase, other things being equal. But there is considerable uncertainty over what the numerical relationship should be between these variables.

For example, many theories of the demand for international reserves suggest that reserves should rise less than in proportion to the increase in the volume of transactions, but both theoretical and empirical studies differ considerably on the actual and predicted deviations from proportionality. Depending on variations in the size of payments disturbances, the costs of adjustment, the availability of loans, and the allocation of reserves, a given degree of reserve ease or stringency could be maintained with a rising or falling ratio of international reserves to international trade.

Nor was there any unambiguous scientific way of determining whether or not the original degree of reserve ease or tightness was desirable. Although technical studies in this area are far from valueless, they could not reasonably be expected to convince the main political disputants that more, or less, rapid expansion of international liquidity was desirable.

An alternative approach would not try to estimate the "correct" growth of international liquidity from demand-for-reserves equa-

---

[13] Recent studies on the demand for international reserves include John F. O. Bilson and Jacob A. Frenkel, "Dynamic Adjustment and the Demand for International Reserves," International Economics Workshop Report No. 7942 (Chicago, Ill.: Department of Economics, University of Chicago, 1979); Peter B. Clark, "Optimum International Reserves and the Speed of Adjustment," Journal of Political Economy, vol. 78, no. 2 (March/April 1970), pp. 356–76; Peter B. Clark, "Demand for International Reserves: A Cross-Country Analysis," Canadian Journal of Economics, vol. 3, no. 1 (November 1970), pp. 577–94; Jacob A. Frenkel, "International Reserves, Pegged Exchange Rates, and Managed Floating," in Karl Brunner and Allan H. Meltzer, eds., Economic Policies in Open Economics, vol. 9 of the Carnegie-Rochester Conference Series on Public Policy, a Supplementary Series to the Journal of Monetary Economics (1978); Jacob A. Frenkel, "International Reserves under Pegged Exchange Rates and Managed Float: Corrections and Extensions," Working Paper (Chicago, Ill.: Department of Economics, University of Chicago, 1979); Jacob A. Frenkel and Boyan Jovanovic, "Optimal International Reserves: A Stochastic Framework," International Economics Workshop Working Paper (Chicago, Ill.: Department of Economics, University of Chicago, 1979); H. Robert Heller and Moskin S. Khan, "The Demand for International Reserves under Fixed and Flexible Exchange Rates," IMF Staff Papers, vol. 25, no. 4 (Washington, D.C.: International Monetary Fund, 1978), pp. 623–49; Michael G. Kelly, "The Demand for International Reserves," American Economic Review, vol. 60, no. 4 (September 1970), pp. 655–67; and John H. Makin, "Reserve Adequacy before and after Limited Floating," Journal of Economics and Business, vol. 30, no. 1 (Fall 1977), pp. 8–14. See also the surveys cited in the preceding footnote.

tions. Instead, this approach would adjust the rate of growth of international liquidity upwards or downwards in line with feedback from the actual operation of the world economy. If a strong preponderance of countries were being forced to devalue or to adopt restrictions or undesirable deflationary policies because of balance-of-payments deficits, then more rapid growth would clearly be needed. If a large preponderance of countries were revaluing their currencies and following inflationary policies, then the rate of growth of international liquidity would need to be reduced.

This is quite a sensible approach. The difficulty is that it gives clear signals only when there are obvious huge imbalances in the aggregate demand and supply for international reserves. In a more normal situation, many countries will display symptoms of reserve deficiencies, while many others may show symptoms of excessive liquidity. In such instances, there are no clear criteria for distinguishing between widespread payments disequilibrium and imbalances in the aggregate demand and supply of international liquidity. The question comes back to the judgmental one of whether, on balance, more or less pressure should be placed on surplus or deficit countries to adjust.

A further deficiency in this control mechanism for aggregate international liquidity is that it can be used to place greater pressures to adjust on surplus countries only by reducing the pressures on deficit countries. One can imagine a case in which it would be judged that surplus countries were not taking enough measures relative to deficit countries, while also concluding that in absolute terms deficit countries were, themselves, not undertaking sufficient adjustment. Indeed, in my own judgment this actually was the case during much of the operation of the Bretton Woods system.

This analysis suggests that coherent management of aggregate international liquidity can play an important role in avoiding potential global excesses or deficiencies of liquidity, but that apart from the avoidance of such extreme situations, it has very little power to fine-tune the efficiency of the operation of the international adjustment process. For such fine-tuning, direct approaches to the international surveillance of the adjustment process are required.

The Reserve Role of the Dollar and the Inefficiency of Adjustment Signaling under the Bretton Woods Gold-Dollar System

The relative inefficiency of international liquidity provisions as a method of controlling the operation of the world economy is further illustrated by considering the operation of the gold-dollar system that

19

actually evolved out of Bretton Woods. So far, we have been treating the stock of international reserves as something that could not be manufactured by individual countries themselves. In other words, the supply of international reserves was exogenously determined through the flow of gold into official coffers and/or collective decisions to create international fiat reserves or borrowing rights.

This has been the traditional assumption of international liquidity studies, but even before the establishment of the Bretton Woods system a portion of official international liquidity was demand-determined in the sense that countries deliberately supplemented their holdings of gold by acquiring holdings of key foreign currencies that could be used to settle payments imbalances. The gold-exchange standard reached its heyday during the operation of the Bretton Woods system, with the dollar becoming the predominant reserve currency. There is some question about the extent to which the emergence of the dollar standard occurred by design. It is clear that it was an objective of Secretary of the Treasury Morgenthau to establish the United States as a major international financial center; it was also clear from the beginning that the dollar would play a special role in the Bretton Woods system. It is doubtful, however, that many of the Bretton Woods negotiators anticipated how much of a dominant role the dollar would take on.

The adjustment pressures operating through international reserve flows under pegged exchange rates operated differently for reserve and nonreserve currency countries. Responsibility for maintaining currency values within a narrow band was placed on the nonreserve currencies. A country with a balance-of-payments surplus would have to buy foreign exchange to keep the exchange value of its currency from rising above legal limits. Likewise, a deficit country would have to sell foreign exchange. With the exception of small groupings of countries which pegged to the French franc and the pound sterling, these obligations were maintained by buying and selling dollars. The ability of a deficit country to maintain the exchange rate of its currency was limited by its holdings of foreign exchange (that is, dollars), its ability to borrow foreign exchange from the International Monetary Fund or elsewhere, and its ability to sell its gold holdings in order to buy dollars.

Adjustment pressures on the reserve center—the United States— were not so direct. The United States did not intervene in the foreign exchange market to maintain exchange rates. Rather, it met its obligations by standing ready to buy and sell freely gold for dollars (at an initial price of $35 per ounce, plus or minus a small handling charge). The Articles of Agreement of the International Monetary

Fund specified that any country could satisfy its obligations under either of these two methods, but the United States was, in fact, the only country to adopt the gold-convertibility method.

When the United States ran a balance-of-payments deficit it did not suffer a direct decline in its reserves as did other countries. Other countries purchased dollars in order to maintain the official pattern of exchange rates. Thus, initially, the United States incurred an increase in its liabilities, rather than a reduction in its reserves. The defense of surplus countries against the continued accumulation of unwanted dollars was their option of converting their dollars into gold, thus draining the U.S. reserve position and placing pressures on the United States to adjust.

Charges that the Bretton Woods system was designed to allow the United States blatantly to exploit financial benefits from its international power position are greatly overstated. In the Bretton Woods system, the United States was not free from adjustment pressures, but these pressures were a step removed from the direct consequences of balance-of-payments deficits that faced the nonreserve countries.

Nor did the United States profit as much from its greater ability to run balance-of-payments deficits as many have charged. It is still not universally recognized that the "seniorage" that the United States earned from the growing accumulations of dollars held abroad was sharply limited by the fact that most of these dollars were held in securities and bank deposits carrying competitive rates of interest, not as zero-interest-bearing cash and demand deposits.[14] Although the United States probably was able to borrow at a cheaper rate than it could have otherwise, it was by no means merely issuing paper IOUs, as charged by General de Gaulle. Nor was this privilege of cheap borrowing entirely at the discretion of the United States. Thus the decisions of other countries could in effect force the United States

---

[14] The view that foreign dollar accumulations were actually held predominantly in cash has been widely held by critics of the U.S. special privilege. Although the empirical invalidity of this view has been pointed out time and again, the frequency with which this view is presented does not appear to have declined; it is still frequently encountered. For a recent example, see Martin Mayer, "The Incredible Shrinking Dollar," *Atlantic Monthly*, vol. 242, no. 2 (August 1978), pp. 59–65. It should also be noted that competition among U.S. financial institutions is sufficient to eliminate most seniorage gains. Only if there were one institution in which dollars could be held would competition from other reserve assets be required for potential monopoly seniorage gains to be substantially reduced. This point is missed in Benjamin J. Cohen's recent discussion of seniorage, *Organizing the World's Money: The Political Economy of International Monetary Relations* (New York: Basic Books, 1977). There is no general agreement on just how much seniorage was left after taking these considerations into account, but it was undoubtedly far less than many popular discussions have assumed.

to borrow when U.S. policy makers might have preferred that this not occur.

Some theorists have argued that reserve currencies should be expected to run international deficits as a way of maximizing government seniorage.[15] As applied to the actual operation of the Bretton Woods system, however, such models tend to overlook two facts. First, the seniorage that could be earned by the U.S. government was greatly limited by the payment of interest on most of these international dollar holdings. Second, the potential gains from such seniorage would rank relatively low in the scale of priorities of the government. Under the Bretton Woods arrangements, the United States had little control over the exchange rate of the dollar. Thus its major method of assuring a balance-of-payments deficit to gain international seniorage would have been to adopt more inflationary domestic policies.

It is true that the ability to gain even limited international seniorage would increase calculations of the optimal inflation tax which a government could levy, but I doubt that among the many factors that influenced the U.S. macroeconomic policies such considerations weighed very heavily.[16] U.S. monetary and fiscal policy over the postwar period has been dominated by domestic macroeconomic objectives. At times when U.S. macroeconomic policies have been specifically concerned with international considerations, these have pressed in the direction of less, rather than more, expansionary policies. For example, one of the major difficulties faced by President Kennedy's advisers in attempting to convince him of the desirability of proposing a tax cut in the early 1960s was the concern that this would worsen the U.S. balance-of-payments deficit. Likewise, one of the major arguments advanced to Congress in support of the 1968 income-tax surcharge was the need to improve the U.S. balance-of-payments deficit.

It is true that, especially after the Kennedy tax cut, the U.S. government was not willing to sacrifice domestic employment by adopting deflationary macroeconomic policies in order to eliminate the U.S. balance-of-payments deficit. Although officials felt concern over the payments deficits run by the United States from the late 1950s to the early 1970s, the implementation of such concerns was

---

[15] See, for example, Robert Mundell, "The Optimum Balance of Payments Deficit," in Emile Classen and Pascal Salin, eds., *Stabilization Policies in Interdependence Economics* (London: North Holland, 1972), pp. 69–86.
[16] On optimal inflation taxes, see Robert J. Gordon, "The Demand and Supply of Inflation," *Journal of Law and Economics*, vol. 18, no. 3 (December 1975), pp. 807–36, and the literature cited there.

limited until 1971 to the adoption of various minor measures to promote exports and reduce foreign payments, such as by reducing duty-free allowances of tourists, and to the eventual adoption of voluntary and then mandatory capital controls.[17] Thus, to a great extent the course of U.S. macroeconomic policies during the operation of the Bretton Woods system was independent of balance-of-payments considerations. The U.S. government neither strove to run a balance-of-payments deficit nor was willing to sacrifice the domestic economy to any extent to the requirements of balance-of-payments equilibrium.

Thus, although it is highly doubtful that the Bretton Woods arrangements induced the export of inflationary pressures from the United States, the mechanism for inducing adjustment pressures on the United States was far from effective. In large part this was due to the deficiencies of the Bretton Woods exchange-rate arrangements. Although these arrangements avoided a repetition of the chaos of the unilateral beggar-thy-neighbor trade and exchange-rate policies of the 1930s, the price of this success was the reinstitution of excessive exchange-rate rigidity, discussed above. This problem applied particularly strongly to the United States, because of the large size of U.S. trade and the special international financial role of the dollar. Even if U.S. officials had reached the point where they were willing to bear the domestic political costs of devaluation, there was serious doubt whether the dollar could be effectively devalued. It was widely assumed, and not just in the United States, that most other countries would follow suit. If they did, an attempt at U.S. devaluation would only generate an economic and financial crisis and would have little net favorable impact on the exchange rate of the dollar against other currencies.

Given this situation, the only other alternative was balance-of-payments controls, a device to which the United States did gradually turn. The prolonged U.S. deficit and resulting drain on the U.S. gold stock did place some adjustment pressures on the United States. The United States may, in fact, have been induced to take as much corrective action as it would have under any set of adjustment signals, given the institutional environment of the Bretton Woods system. It is clear in retrospect, however, that the actual system of adjustment

---

[17] An interest equalization tax was also imposed on the purchase of foreign securities. For a more detailed review of the history of U.S. balance-of-payments measures over this period, see Gottfried Haberler and Thomas D. Willett, *U.S. Balance of Payments Policies and International Monetary Reform* (Washington, D.C.: American Enterprise Institute, 1968). Balance-of-payments reasons were used by the administration as one of the justifications to Congress for the 1968 tax surcharge, but this was primarily a convenient, additional rationale for what the administration wanted to do anyway for domestic reasons.

signals provided was seriously defective. It did not provide an efficient mechanism for allocating adjustment responsibilities.

In part, this was due initially to the very attractiveness of holding dollars. As was indicated above, official dollar holdings paid competitive rates of interest. On the other hand, gold holdings carried a positive cost for storage and insurance. As long as free convertibility between dollars and gold at a fixed price was assured, there were strong incentives for countries to hold dollars rather than gold. During the first years of the operation of the Bretton Woods system, the dollar was not as good as gold—it was better.

A surplus country thus had a conflict between portfolio balance and adjustment signaling incentives.[18] Although such a country might prefer the United States to take actions to reduce the size of the payments imbalance, it might not want to convert its dollars into gold, especially if its individual purchase of gold would not be likely to have a strong effect on U.S. policies. When gold conversions did occur, they could be for reasons unconnected to changes in the state of overall payments imbalances. For reasons of tradition and law and different evaluations of portfolio balance considerations, some countries tended to hold a high proportion of their reserves in gold while other countries tended to hold a low proportion. A change in the composition of surplus countries could then lead the United States to gain or lose gold while the overall size of the U.S. payments deficit remained unchanged. For both of these reasons, the actual magnitude of gold conversions could not be taken as a good indicator of the aggregate amount of disequilibrium between the reserve center and nonreserve countries.

The Interrelationship of International Liquidity and Confidence Problems: The Triffin Dilemma

The inefficiency of the gold adjustment signaling was further heightened by the emergence of the liquidity-confidence dilemma of the Bretton Woods system that was so brilliantly diagnosed by Robert Triffin.[19] Triffin pointed out in the late 1950s that the Bretton Woods system could not go on operating as it had. Most of the expansion in international liquidity had come from increased foreign official

---

[18] See Lawrence H. Officer and Thomas D. Willett, "Reserve-Asset Preferences and the Confidence Problem in the Crisis Zone," *Quarterly Journal of Economics*, vol. 83, no. 4 (November 1969), pp. 688–95, and "The Interaction of Adjustment and Gold Conversion Policies in a Reserve-Currency System," *Western Economic Journal*, vol. 8 (March 1970), pp. 47–60.

[19] See Robert Triffin, *Gold and the Dollar Crisis* (New Haven, Conn.: Yale University Press, 1960).

holdings of dollars. At the beginning of the operation of the system there were few outstanding dollar balances abroad and the major portion of global official gold reserves resided in the United States. The international liquidity provisions of the Bretton Woods system had been based on the assumption that new gold production would be adequate to meet most of the needs for growth in international liquidity over time. These projections turned out to be much too optimistic, in part because of the unforeseen burst of world inflation that followed World War II and substantially reduced the real value of the fixed nominal price of gold. Provisions had been made to meet a future scarcity of gold through an increase in its price—that is, a uniform devaluation of all currencies—but the operation of this provision became ruled out in practice. The quotas of the International Monetary Fund were like a pool of national funds that could be borrowed by deficit countries under certain conditions.[20] Thus they increased the liquidity of the system, but did not represent owned reserves in the manner of gold; expansions of fund quotas were not viewed as a method of increasing international liquidity on which exclusive reliance could be placed.

Thus it had been fortunate for the operation of the system during the 1950s that countries had desired to accumulate a large part of their balance-of-payments surpluses in the form of increased dollar holdings rather than through draining the gold reserves of the United States. This process was reaching its limits, however. As Triffin pointed out, outstanding official dollar holdings were becoming large relative to their backing—the U.S. gold stock.[21] The growth in dollar holdings relative to gold backing could not continue indefinitely without calling into doubt the continued free convertibility of the dollar into gold.

Because conversions of dollar accumulations into gold were not automatic, there was considerable uncertainty as to just how many dollars abroad could be supported by a given size of U.S. gold stock without generating a run on the world's bank. Continued reliance on dollar acceleration to meet the growth of international liquidity, however, ran an increasing risk that a collapse of, or at least a change in, the operation of the system would be required. On the other hand, limiting dollar accumulations to amounts that could unquestionably

---

[20] For discussions of the International Monetary Fund's quotas and international lending operations, see International Monetary Fund, "The Fund under the Second Amendment: A Supplement," *IMF Survey* (September 18, 1978).

[21] For much of this period, the entire U.S. gold stock was not available for international backing, as a substantial portion was for some time required to back the U.S. money supply. The ratios of gold backing for both domestic and international liabilities were progressively reduced and eventually eliminated.

be supported by the U.S. gold stock would soon generate a shortage of international liquidity. Thus the system faced a basic dilemma. Without some change a crisis of confidence or a liquidity shortage would result.

The Failure of the SDR Reform

This analysis presented the intellectual underpinnings of the efforts to create a new source of international liquidity growth that culminated in the establishment of special drawing rights (SDRs).[22] As it turned out, however, the creation of SDRs was neither necessary nor sufficient to maintain the original provisions of the Bretton Woods system. The dollar had already become de facto inconvertible into gold for large purchases by major dollar holders before SDRs were created. A collapse of the structure of the monetary system was avoided by a de facto limitation on the operations of the gold adjustment signaling mechanism. Despite the considerable uncertainties generated by the looseness of the gold conversion mechanism, a combination of luck and interest in preserving the status quo by the major dollar holders brought the system into a more stable position. Dollars outstanding exceeded the U.S. gold backing by so much that it was clear to the major dollar holders that if any followed France in its "war on the dollar" and converted dollars into gold, this would generate a major run on the dollar.

Given the relatively small number of major dollar holders and their great aversion to running the risk of upsetting the status quo, these countries were willing to absorb more dollars than they wanted, without attempting to convert them into gold. According to the analysis of Officer and Willett,[23] as long as the rate of foreign official dollar accumulation was not far in excess of demands, the Bretton Woods system could have continued indefinitely without the need for formal revision. In other words, as long as a large part of any U.S. deficit

[22] For discussions of the SDR negotiations, see Stephen D. Cohen, *International Monetary Reform, 1964–69: The Political Dimension* (New York: Praeger, 1970); Fritz Machlup, *Remaking the International Monetary System* (Baltimore, Md.: Johns Hopkins University Press, 1968); Robert Solomon, *The International Monetary System* (New York: Harper and Row, 1977); and Susan Strange, *International Monetary Relations* (London: Oxford University Press, 1976).

[23] See Officer and Willett, "Reserve-Asset Preferences," pp. 688–95, and "Adjustment and Gold Conversion Policies," pp. 47–60. See also the subsequent studies by Fred Hirsch, "SDRs and the Working of the Gold Exchange Standard," *IMF Staff Papers*, vol. 18, no. 2 (Washington, D.C.: International Monetary Fund, 1971), pp. 221–53; pp. 221–53; John H. Makin, "On the Success of the Reserve Currency System in the Crisis Zone," *Journal of International Economics*, vol 2 (February 1972), pp. 77–85; and Lawrence H. Officer, "Reserve Asset Preferences in the Crisis Zone, 1958–67," *Journal of Money, Credit, and Banking*, vol. 6, no. 2 (May 1974), pp. 191–213.

was caused by foreign demands rather than excess supply from the United States, the recognition of mutual interdependence among the major central banks would probably have been sufficient to suspend the operation of the Triffin dilemma.

Thus, although the dollar remained legally convertible into gold, and was in fact convertible for the small transactions of nonmajor countries, it became de facto inconvertible with respect to the dollar holdings of the major industrial countries. This de facto inconvertibility provided a shock absorber that increased the stability of the system, but at the cost of almost completely eliminating the adjustment signaling device built into the Bretton Woods system for the reserve currency country. While workable, this could hardly be considered a fully satisfactory system.

And, had it been coupled with U.S attempts to keep other countries from adjusting exchange rates, this system would have been indefensible. The United States did not take such a position, however. Instead, it argued that because of its role in the system it was handicapped in undertaking exchange-rate adjustments and urged other countries to make exchange-rate adjustments if they were accumulating more dollars than they desired. Likewise, the United States was an early advocate of introducing greater exchange-rate flexibility into the system to make it easier for other countries to shield themselves from unwanted dollar accumulations.

A strong case can be made that such a system would make economic sense, but other countries were hesitant to accept such a change in the functioning of the system; the debate over who should adjust to mutual imbalances continued.[24] At the same time, there was debate over how much of the continuing U.S. deficit represented a genuine balance-of-payments disequilibrium and how much represented an equilibrium deficit resulting from meeting the demands of other countries to increase their international reserve holdings over time.[25] The creation of SDRs could eliminate the equilibrium part of the deficit, but this was not what was causing major pressures on the system. SDRs could do nothing about the disequilibrium part of the U.S. deficit.[26]

---

[24] For references to the literature on this subject, see Willett, *Floating Exchange Rates*, chap. 3. Advocates of such a passive U.S. role included Gottfried Haberler, Lawrence Krause, Ronald I. McKinnon, Thomas D. Willett, and Paul Wonnacott.

[25] The classic analysis of how the role of the United States as a world banker could give rise to measured payments deficits that did not represent a genuine disequilibrium was presented in Emile Depres, Charles P. Kindleberger, and Walter S. Salant, "The Dollar and World Liquidity: A Minority View," *The Economist*, vol. 218 (February 1966), pp. 526–29.

[26] The equilibrium and disequilibrium parts of the U.S. deficits were sometimes referred to as demand- and supply-determined deficits, respectively.

One can make a good case for having demands for the growth of international liquidity over time be met by a deliberately created international reserve asset, rather than by increased holdings of the dollar, but the SDR reform did not really bring a major increase in international control over the expansion of international liquidity. It could do nothing to deter aggregate increases in the demands for reserves that were greater than the rate of SDR creation, nor could it deter the more serious problem of an increase in supply-determined international liquidity emanating from U.S. payments deficits.

The former problem could have caused serious problems if genuine convertibility of the dollar into reserve assets had been reestablished, for in that case any increase in reserve assets less than the growth in aggregate demand for reserves could have fed back disproportionately to the United States. This was a major concern of U.S. negotiators during the later efforts to reform the international monetary system in 1973–1974 after the Bretton Woods structure had broken down.

The latter problem was what caused the breakdown of the system. The efforts to finance the Vietnam war without an increase in taxes overheated the U.S. economy and increased the size of the U.S. payments deficit. While masked somewhat by tight money during 1969, the deterioration in the U.S. trade position was soon followed and then magnified by a deterioration in the overall balance of payments. The deterioration in the underlying payments position was accompanied by capital outflows motivated by anticipation of revaluations of the strong foreign currencies and even by fears of an eventual devaluation of the dollar or collapse of the whole pegged exchange-rate structure. Although official settlements deficits of $1 billion to $3 billion per year had been the cause of worries in the past, the U.S. deficit ballooned to almost $10 billion in 1970 and accelerated further during 1971.

It is doubtful that any system without a great deal of exchange-rate flexibility could have avoided such a situation, although a system with better adjustment signals might have helped to generate a move toward greater exchange-rate flexibility more rapidly. The consequent explosion of international liquidity clearly had an adverse effect on the world economy, transmitting inflationary pressures from the United States to the rest of the world. This certainly is a case in which deficiencies in the organization of the international monetary system combined with an episode of instability in a major economy to generate inflationary pressures abroad.

It is open to question how alternative adjustable pegged-rate systems would have operated under the enormous pressures of the overheating of the U.S economy. My guess is that none would have survived these pressures, but that a more symmetrical system that required asset settlements for U.S. deficits might have forced the adoption of exchange-rate flexibility sooner.

This explosion in international liquidity continued throughout the efforts to restore a new structure of pegged exchange rates in 1972 and 1973. This was a case in which large reserve increases, because they were undesired, clearly placed inflationary pressures on the recipient countries as would be predicted from international reserve monetarist views. It is important to remember, however, that this destabilizing supply-determined explosion of international liquidity was the result of the death throes of the old pegged exchange-rate system. As will be reviewed below, the consequences of "uncontrolled" reserve increases under flexible exchange rates may be quite different.

Although fears are often expressed that under our current flexible-rate system international liquidity is demand determined, it must be remembered that this was also the case under the Bretton Woods pegged-rate system as well. It was not the demand-determined component of international liquidity expansion that caused major problems, it was the supply-determined portion. (The fears of demand-determined expansion of international liquidity will be considered in more detail below.) Thus it is not legitimate to take the 1970–1972 international liquidity explosion as an example of the instabilities that can be generated by an uncontrolled demand-determined international liquidity mechanism under our new international monetary arrangements based on flexible exchange rates.

The Effects of the International Liquidity Explosion of 1970–1972

Even in the case of this destabilizing supply-determined splurge of international liquidity expansion between 1970 and 1972, the effects on world inflationary pressures were not nearly as great as many international reserve monetarists have argued. The use of aggregate statistics in many of these monetarist studies has led to a greatly exaggerated impression of the magnitude of inflationary pressures generated by the 1970–1972 international liquidity explosion.

Investigations of the relationships between the growth of international reserves and the rate of growth of the sum of the money supplies of the major industrial countries other than the United States led the authors of several studies to conclude, not unreasonably, that the international liquidity explosion was the dominant explanation of the accompanying rapid acceleration in the growth of the money supplies in these countries.[27] The aggregate facts were thus in accord with the prediction of the international reserve monetarist theories, and these authors saw little need to search for further explanations.

In subsequent analysis, however, it turned out that this apparent strong relationship did not hold up well on a country-by-country basis. There was little correlation between the countries that received the largest reserve increases and those that showed the most rapid accelerations in their rates of monetary expansion.[28] This lack of relationship suggested that a considerable portion of the aggregate acceleration in monetary growth may have resulted from domestic causes that happened to coincide with the explosion of international liquidity.

Further recent research has found results consistent with this latter hypothesis. As part of a study on the causes of monetary expansion in the major industrial countries, Leroy Laney and I have estimated policy reaction functions for the monetary authorities of these countries.[29] These reaction functions include both domestic variables, such as budget deficits and wage increases, and international variables, such as import prices and international reserve changes.

Using these estimates, we calculated how much of the monetary expansion in each country between 1970 and 1972 was due to international reserve increases and how much was due to domestic factors. As is indicated in table 1, of the eleven countries investigated, only for Germany, the Netherlands, and Switzerland did domestic considerations fail to explain the majority of the expansions of narrowly defined money stocks. For the group as a whole, domestic factors accounted for 68 to 72 percent of the aggregate rate of increase, depending upon the weights used in the aggregation and whether narrowly or broadly defined money supply figures were used. The direct estimates of the effects of reserve increases accounted for only 11 to 18 percent of the aggregate money supply increases.

[27] See Henry Goldstein, "Monetary Policy under Fixed and Floating Rates," National Westminster Bank *Quarterly Review* (November 1974), pp. 15–27; H. Robert Heller, "International Reserves and Worldwide Inflation," *IMF Staff Papers*, vol. 23, no. 1 (Washington , D.C.: International Monetary Fund, 1976), pp. 61–87; Michael K. Keran, "Towards an Explanation of Simultaneous Inflation-Recession," San Francisco Federal Reserve Bank *Business Review* (Spring 1975), pp. 18–30; and D. I. Meiselman and A. B. Laffer, eds., *The Phenomenon of Worldwide Inflation* (Washington, D.C.: American Enterprise Institute, 1975).

[28] See Thomas D. Willett, "The Eurocurrency Market, Exchange-Rate Systems, and National Financial Policies," in Carl Stem, John Makin, and Dennis Logue, eds., *Eurocurrencies and the International Monetary System* (Washington, D.C.: American Enterprise Institute, 1976), pp. 193–221.

[29] See Leroy Laney and Thomas D. Willett, "The International Liquidity Explosion and Worldwide Monetary Expansion: 1970–1972," Claremont Working Papers (Claremont, Calif.: Claremont Graduate School, 1980).

TABLE 1

CAUSES OF MONETARY GROWTH DURING THE INTERNATIONAL LIQUIDITY EXPLOSION, 1970–1972

	Narrow Money Stock				Broad Money Stock			
	%M	H	R	Rᵁ	%M	H	R	Rᵁ
Australia	10.07	9.36	3.48	3.48	11.17	9.55	2.22	2.22
Belgium	11.13	9.56	2.60	2.60	12.60	11.82	1.01	1.01
Canada	9.03	5.56	*	3.47	11.23	18.89	*	*
France	12.60	7.83	2.10	4.77	17.33	6.37	1.62	10.96
Germany	12.10	5.97	0.19	6.13	13.93	0.34	*	13.59
Italy	21.23	13.20	0.43	8.03	16.47	14.34	0.04	2.13
Japan	23.73	19.76	6.80	6.80	21.97	17.76	5.54	5.54
Netherlands	14.83	4.88	8.16	9.95	13.80	7.06	6.66	6.74
Sweden	8.77	5.82	*	2.95	9.33	8.96	0.02	0.37
Switzerland	11.37	0.23	6.24	11.14	10.33	1.35	4.33	8.98
United Kingdom	12.37	11.90	1.08	1.08	16.83	17.80	0.36	0.36

Totals:
  1. Aggregate average
  rate of monetary growth
    a. Weighted by money

	%M	H	R	Rᵁ	%M	H	R	Rᵁ
stock changes	18.40	13.18	3.39	6.31	17.61	12.31	2.66	6.23

  b. Weighted by real
  GNP

	15.12	10.50	2.50	5.32	16.08	11.02	1.83	6.17

  2. Proportion of
  aggregate monetary
  growth estimated due to
  each factor
    a. Weighted by money
    stock changes

		0.72	0.18	0.34		0.70	0.15	0.35

  b. Weighted by real
  GNP

		0.69	0.17	0.35		0.69	0.11	0.38

NOTES:
%M = Average annual rate of monetary growth
H = Estimate of average rate of monetary growth due to domestic factor
R = Estimate of average rate of monetary growth due to international reserve changes
Rᵁ = Upper bound estimate of average rate of monetary growth due to reserve increases (equals R plus any positive residuals from estimating equations)
*When the estimated reserve coefficient in the regression is negative, the contribution of reserve changes to monetary expansion is constrained to be equal to zero.

SOURCE: Leroy Laney and Thomas D. Willett, "The International Liquidity Explosion and Worldwide Monetary Expansion: 1970–1972," Claremont Working Papers (Claremont, Calif.: Claremont Graduate School, 1980). The methodology for these estimates is presented in Leroy Laney and Thomas D. Willett, "Monetarism, Budget Deficits, and Wage Push Inflation: The Cases of Italy and the United Kingdom," Banca Nazionale del Lavoro, *Quarterly Review*, no. 128 (December 1978), pp. 315–31.

Of course, any particular set of such estimates cannot be definitive, and alternative specifications of the equations and inclusion of different domestic variables would undoubtedly lead to somewhat different empirical results. I suspect that subsequent studies are unlikely to upset the basic picture offered by these results, however.

The supply-determined increases in international liquidity in 1970–1972 undoubtedly did contribute to more rapid global monetary expansion than would otherwise have been the case; the amounts of these effects were not trivial. But for most countries, higher rates of monetary expansion would have occurred for domestic reasons anyway, and many countries have considerable ability, at least in the short run, to sterilize most of the effects of undesired international reserve inflows on domestic monetary aggregates.

Systematic empirical studies tend to suggest that many countries have displayed much greater abilities to sterilize the effects of monetary inflows than is often implied by the statements of monetary officials. Table 2 shows the results of a number of these studies. A negative sign on the estimates in the table indicates that the domestic component of the monetary base has varied to offset the effects of variations in the foreign component of the base caused by reserve inflows or outflows. A coefficient of -1 indicates complete offsetting.[30] Again, these estimates should not be taken as definitive and variations appear among the specific results of various studies. Taken together, however, they indicate that many countries do have considerable ability to insulate their money supplies from international capital and reserve flows in the short run even under pegged exchange rates. Indeed, as is indicated in table 3, these studies suggest

[30] Early studies in this area did not attempt to distinguish between the effects of international capital flows offsetting the effects of a tightening or a loosening of domestic monetary policy and the effects of sterilization of reserve inflows. Initial findings of a high negative correlation between the domestic and the foreign components of the monetary base were therefore interpreted by some as evidence of high monetary interdependence, with international capital flows swamping the efforts of national monetary authorities to alter domestic monetary conditions; the same results were interpreted by others as an indication of a higher degree of national monetary control, which could offset the domestic effects of international disturbances. The solution to this controversy was an attempt to identify when developments were due to desired changes in the money supply and when they were due to exogenous international disturbances. This was done by estimating reaction functions for the domestic monetary authorities. All of the results reported in table 2 come from second-generation studies that attempt to identify the causes of disturbance in this manner. For further discussion on this point, see Victor Argy and Penti Kouri, "Sterilization Policies and the Volatility in International Reserves," in Robert Z. Aliber, ed., *National Monetary Policies and the International Financial System* (Chicago, Ill.: University of Chicago Press, 1974); and Richard J. Sweeney and Thomas D. Willett, "The International Transmission of Inflation," in Michele Fratianni and Karel Tavevnier, eds., *Bank Credit, Money, and Inflation in Open Economies*, A Special Supplement to *Kredit und Kapital*, Heft 3 (1976), pp. 441–517.

even smaller effects from the 1970–1972 liquidity explosion than did the Laney-Willett estimates.

Of course, not all countries can sterilize reserve inflows. It has been argued that a few smaller industrial countries actually used their balance of payments as a means of controlling the rate of domestic monetary growth, using variations in administrative procedures and the like to induce a surplus if they wanted to increase the rate of monetary expansion and to induce a deficit if they wanted to slow the rate of monetary growth.[31] Such countries were quite susceptible to the adverse effects of international liquidity supply shocks. It is interesting to note that many of those practitioners and officials most sympathetic to international reserve monetarist views come from the smaller European countries that have the least scope for monetary independence.

Thus views on the international liquidity mechanism are often strongly influenced by extrapolation from the conditions of one's home economy. The same has held with respect to views on the relative desirability of fixed versus flexible exchange rates. The theory of optimum currency areas suggests that flexible rates will tend to be more attractive for relatively large economies while fixed rates have greater relative attractiveness for small open economies. The views of both academicians and officials in this debate have not been entirely uncorrelated with the characteristics of their home economies.[32] A large liquidity supply shock, such as occurred in 1970–1972, will undoubtedly force some countries to inflate more rapidly, but the effects are likely to vary greatly from one country to another. This is likewise true of the other mechanisms through which reserve increases may ultimately cause more expansionary policies.

Alternative Views of the Demand for International Reserves

One popular view of the role of international reserves is quite similar to some versions of Keynesian, as opposed to monetarist, monetary theory. In domestic monetarist theory, excess demands and supplies of money motivate economic behavior equally. In some versions of

[31] See, for example, Samuel I. Katz, *External Surpluses, Capital Flows, and Credit Policy in the European Economic Community*, Princeton Studies in International Finance, no. 22 (Princeton, N.J.: International Finance Section, Princeton University, 1969).

[32] The theory of optimum currency areas was named by Robert Mundell, although some of its basic elements had been identified in earlier literature. For discussions of the subsequent development of this approach, and for references to the literature, see Edward Tower and Thomas D. Willett, "The Theory of Optimum Currency Areas and Exchange Rate Flexibility," Special Papers in International Economics, no. 11 (Princeton, N.J.: International Finance Section, Princeton University, 1976).

TABLE 2
STERILIZATION COEFFICIENT ESTIMATES

Author(s)	Country	Frequency & Interval	Estimates
Argy & Kouri (1974)	Germany	Q: 1963:3–1970:4	$-0.34\left(\frac{\text{current}}{\text{account}}\right); -0.19\left(\frac{\text{capital}}{\text{account}}\right)$
	Italy	Q: 1964:1–1970:4	$-1.37\left(\frac{\text{current}}{\text{account}}\right); -0.67\left(\frac{\text{capital}}{\text{account}}\right)$
	Netherlands	Q: 1964:1–1970:4	$-0.74\left(\frac{\text{current}}{\text{account}}\right); -0.87\left(\frac{\text{capital}}{\text{account}}\right)$
Artus (1975)	Germany	M; 1973:4–1975:7	−0.745
Herring & Marston (1977)	Germany	Q: 1960:1–1969:2	−0.91
Hickman & Schleicher (1978)	Australia	A; 1958–1976	−0.83
	Belgium	A; 1958–1976	−0.68
	Canada	A; 1958–1976	−1.09
	France	A; 1958–1976	−1.56
	Germany	A; 1958–1976	−0.61
	Italy	A; 1958–1976	−1.43
	Japan	A; 1958–1976	−1.22
	Netherlands	A; 1958–1976	−0.89
	Sweden	A; 1958–1976	−1.40
	Switzerland	A; 1958–1976	−0.39
	United Kingdom	A; 1958–1976	−1.23

Laney (1978)	Australia	M; 1966:1–1977:8	−0.81
	Belgium	M; 1964:2–1977:6	−0.69
	Canada	M; 1963:1–1977:11	−1.00
	France	M; 1963:8–1977:9	−1.20
	Germany	M; 1964:2–1977:9	−0.68
	Italy	M; 1966:2–1977:10	−0.83
	Japan	M; 1966:3–1977:10	−1.69
	Netherlands	M; 1958:1–1977:11	−0.80
	Sweden	M; 1962:8–1977:5	−1.13
	Switzerland	M; 1963:4–1977:6	−0.07
	United Kingdom	M; 1964:1–1977:2	−1.31
Miller (1976)	Canada	Q; 1960:1–1969:4	−1.10
	Germany	Q; 1960:1–1969:4	−0.979
	Japan	Q; 1960:1–1969:4	−0.538
	United Kingdom	Q; 1960:1–1969:4	−1.02
Willms (1971)	Germany	Q; 1958:1–1970:2	−0.863

NOTE: See text for explanation of sign of coefficients. Q = quarterly; M = monthly; A = annually.

SOURCE: Laney and Willett, "International Liquidity Explosion."

TABLE 3

CALCULATIONS OF THE MONETARY EFFECTS OF THE INTERNATIONAL
LIQUIDITY EXPLOSION, 1970–1972, BASED ON ESTIMATES OF
STERILIZATION COEFFICIENTS

	Using Narrow Definition of Money (M_1)				Using Broad Definition of Money (M_2)			
	$\%M_1$	S_H	S_L	S_A	$\%M_2$	S_H	S_L	S_A
Australia	10.07	6.93	7.70	7.32	11.17	6.89	7.79	7.34
Belgium	11.13	3.59	3.71	3.65	12.60	3.62	3.74	3.68
Canada	9.03	*	*	*	11.23	*	*	*
France	12.60	*	*	*	17.33	*	*	*
Germany	12.10	0.5	10.91	5.58	13.93	0.5	11.18	5.72
Italy	21.23	*	0.25	0.13	16.47	*	0.23	0.12
Japan	23.73	*	11.27	5.64	21.97	*	11.03	5.52
Netherlands	14.83	*	4.41	2.21	13.80	*	*	2.19
Sweden	8.77	*	*	*	9.33	*	*	*
Switzerland	11.37	8.29	12.64	10.47	10.33	8.12	12.37	10.25
United Kingdom	12.37	*	*	*	16.83	*	*	*
Totals								
1. Aggregate average rate of monetary growth								
a. Weighted by money stock changes	18.40	0.45	5.67	3.06	17.61	0.51	6.55	3.51
b. Weighted by real GNP	15.12	0.61	5.20	2.88	16.08	0.61	5.20	2.88
2. Proportion of aggregate monetary growth estimated due to each factor								
a. Weighted by money stock changes		0.02	0.31	0.17		0.03	0.37	0.20
b. Weighted by real GNP		0.04	0.34	0.19		0.04	0.32	0.18

NOTES:

$\%M$ = Average annual rate of monetary growth

S_H = Average annual rate of monetary growth due to international reserve increases based on highest estimates of sterilization coefficients (those in table 2)

S_L = Average annual rate of monetary growth due to international reserve increases based on lowest estimates of sterilization coefficients

S_A = Average annual rate of monetary growth due to international reserve increases based on average of estimates of sterilization coefficients

* When the average, high, or low surveyed sterilization coefficient exceeds minus unity, international reserve flows are assumed to be completely sterilized.

SOURCE: Laney and Willett, "International Liquidity Explosion."

Keynesian theory, however, the money supply is considered to be more like a constraint than a behavioral variable. This view is illustrated by the old analogy between monetary policy and a string: Tight money can hold back the economy but easy money cannot push it forward. Such behavior would characterize an economy if it were in Keynes's famous liquidity trap.

Modern research has tended to discount the empirical importance of this condition as applied to the relationship between money supplies and the behavior of domestic economies. As a description of the relationships between international reserve changes and the behavior of governments, this view becomes much more plausible, however.[33] National governments have much weaker incentives to achieve optimal reserve holdings than firms have to achieve optimal holdings of money balances. In some respects for many industrial countries the demand for international reserves would be analogous to the demand for money by a wealthy individual who manages his own money. Except when he or she is running out of it, the wealthy person might pay little attention to the level of his or her cash balances. In technical terms, we would say that over a wide range there would be little change in the marginal utility of additions to or subtractions from the level of money balances. Only when money balances dropped very low would variations in the level become important. A similar case would apply to government officials in wealthy industrial countries whose main concern was achieving domestic macroeconomic objectives. In each case, the demand for money or demand for reserve functions would be like that depicted in figure 1. The steep portion of the curve at low reserve levels would approximate the view of reserves acting primarily as a constraint.

Concern for money balances or international reserves would constrain spending or induce other adjustments when reserves were very short, for example, at point *a*, but at higher levels reserves would have very little effect on behavior. This lack of effect would not reflect irrational or nonmaximizing behavior; it would simply mean that variations in the utility generated by increases or decreases in reserve levels would be low relative to the costs that would be required to adjust reserves. For a country under adjustable pegged exchange rates, exchange-rate adjustments or changes in macroeconomic policies necessary to acquire or get rid of reserves would be viewed as being more costly than deviations from optimal reserve levels over

---

[33] Walter Salant has argued, for example, that "global reserves are less an instrument closely geared to a target variable than a potential constraint on the attainment of targets." Walter S. Salant, "Practical Techniques for Assessing the Need for World Reserves," in *International Reserves*, p. 304.

a wide range (*ob* to *oc* in figure 1). In such cases, as long as a country was able to sterilize the domestic monetary effects of reserve flows, there could be a wide range over which accumulations or losses of reserves would not influence economic behavior.[34] Of course, private entities also have such thresholds with respect to adjusting their financial positions, but these thresholds are likely to be of much less aggregate importance for predicting the relationships between money supply changes and private behavior than for predicting relationships between changes in international reserves and national behavior. This is both because of the lesser scope for the law of large numbers to operate in, in the latter case, and because of the relatively low place of optimal financial positions in the hierarchy of government concerns.

Again, this situation need not be caused by irrational or non-maximizing behavior. It is based on recognition that there is more than one factor in officials' demand for reserve functions. The range of inaction in response to reserve changes is also likely to be substantially widened because financial officials are likely to view economic adjustments as being much more costly in political terms than they are in terms of the aggregate economic effects on the economy. Especially with the use of exchange-rate changes under the adjustable peg, officials tended to view adjustments as being much more costly than did most economists. This status quo bias was undoubtedly influenced to some extent by the general tendency of most political officials to be less enthusiastic about the use of the price system than most economists. To a large extent, however, it reflected rational short-run political views that such adjustments might be particularly costly in political terms to those initiating them. Personal prestige would often be damaged and there was a not unreasonable suspicion that those who were adversely affected by the change in exchange rates would react more strongly politically than those who gained from it.

---

[34] The reserve levels in figure 1 should be thought of as expected average levels and would not correspond to actual reserve holdings at all times. Thus, if a reserve increase were expected to be reversed soon, this increase would not cause an outward movement on the *DD* schedule.

It should also be noted that we are dealing with international reserves being held primarily for purposes of balance-of-payments financing and exchange-rate maintenance. The normal assumption is that, apart from this contribution, international reserves will earn a lower rate of return than alternative uses of the nation's capital stock. This is a reasonable assumption for most of the industrial and developing countries, but it would not apply to many of the OPEC countries for which a considerable portion of their official reserves reflects investment rather than traditional international reserve considerations; thus, a country like Saudi Arabia would hold a much higher level of international reserves than would make sense on balance-of-payments and exchange-rate grounds.

FIGURE 1
COSTS OF ADJUSTMENT AND THE DEMAND FOR INTERNATIONAL RESERVES

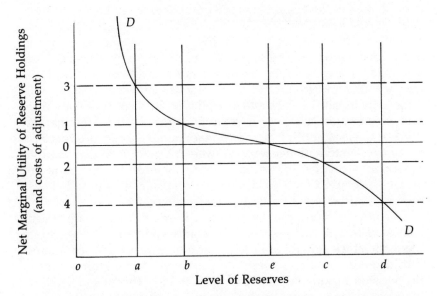

NOTE: This *DD* curve is drawn net of the opportunity costs of holding reserves. Thus point *e*, where marginal utility is zero, represents the economic optimum. The opportunity costs of holding reserves are reduced by the fact that most reserve holdings yield interest earnings. On portfolio or asset balance grounds, however, the opportunity costs of reserve holdings would begin to increase after some point as more and more of total national assets were being held in this form.

Thus underlying figure 1 would be schedules of gross benefits and opportunity costs from reserve holdings, which look like the following:

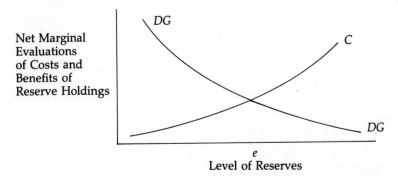

Note that the costs on the vertical axis of figure 1 are adjustment, not interest rate, opportunity costs per se, which are usually shown in typical demand-for-money diagrams. The figure is not meant to imply that the demand for reserves is highly elastic with respect to the interest rate.

39

It is well known from public-choice theory that information and organization costs, incentives to free riding, etc., can lead to considerable biases in the operation of the political process. In such circumstances, Adam Smith's "invisible hand" will not work well. Incentives for individual maximization will differ from those necessary for collective maximization, and aggregate inefficiencies will result. Thus in a manner analogous to the prevalence of protectionist measures that benefit some groups at the expense of aggregate economic efficiency, there can be substantial politically rational deviations from economic optimality in international financial policies.[35] It is hard to think of an election being lost or a finance minister being fired because a country's international reserves were 50 percent higher than an economic calculation of optimal reserve holdings, but there are numerous instances of job loss for finance ministers who presided over exchange-rate changes under the adjustable peg.[36]

In terms of figure 1, if we consider the original cost of adjustment lines at 01 and 02 to have been based on considerations of aggregate economic efficiency, then these political or bureaucratic self-interest considerations would increase the perceived costs of adjustment to the decision-making officials, say to 03 and 04. This would lengthen the reserve range over which economic adjustments would not be induced. Over this extended range it would be likely that the *DD* curve would be falling at a more gradual pace at the upper end than it would be rising at the lower end. As a consequence, the range of inaction would be likely to be expanded to a greater extent on the upper end than on the lower end—that is, *cd* > *ab*.

This would tend to reduce the number of adjustment measures undertaken by surplus countries relative to deficit countries. From the perspective of this constraint view of international reserves, an increase in the supply of international liquidity would loosen the constraints placed on deficit or low-reserve countries. Thus some

---

[35] On the application of public choice analysis to the demand for international reserves and to trade policy, see Ryan C. Amacher, Robert D. Tollison, and Thomas D. Willett, "Risk Avoidance and Political Advertising: Neglected Issues in the Literature on Budget Size in a Democracy," in Ryan C. Amacher, Robert D. Tollison, and Thomas D. Willett, eds., *The Economic Approach to Public Policy* (Ithaca, N.Y.: Cornell University Press, 1976), pp. 405–33; Ryan C. Amacher, Robert D. Tollison, and Thomas D. Willett, "The Divergence between (Trade) Theory and Practice," in Walter Adams et al., *Tariffs, Quotas, and Trade: The Politics of Protectionism* (San Francisco, Calif.: Institute for Contemporary Studies, 1979), pp. 55–66; Edward Tower and Thomas D. Willett, "More on Official versus Market Financing of Payments Deficits and the Optimal Pricing of International Reserves," *Kyklos*, fasc. 3 (1972), pp. 537–52; and Willett, "Public Choice Approach to International Economic Relations."
[36] See, for example, Richard N. Cooper, *Currency Devaluation in Developing Countries*, Princeton Essays in International Finance, no. 86 (Princeton, N.J.: International Finance Section, Princeton University, 1971).

countries would be allowed to undertake more expansionary policies, which they would have liked to undertake anyway but had been constrained from undertaking because of a weak international financial position. Such a situation would apply to perhaps a majority of the less developed countries that do not export oil, and at times to particular industrial countries as well. For countries not in this constrained position, however, reserve increases might have no influence at all on economic behavior, at least initially. Countries in this position have been called "reserve sinks." The initial inflationary effects of an increase of a given size in international reserves could, therefore, vary greatly, depending upon what proportion went to reserve sinks and what proportion went to countries that had relatively little ability to sterilize reserve inflows or were in a reserve-constrained position.

Similarly the "adequacy" of any given aggregate level of reserves could depend on how it is distributed. Mechanical indicators of reserve totals in relation to the volume of world trade—or even more sophisticated indicators, such as measures of payments variability—cannot be considered adequate guides for the supervision of the operation of the international adjustment process. There is far too much slippage possible between reserve totals and the adjustment pressures generated by international liquidity effects.

Reserve Sinks and Second-Round Effects. Uncertainties about the effects of a given change in international reserves are further increased when the second-round effects of international liquidity creation are considered. The fact that reserves may initially flow into a reserve sink does not necessarily mean these reserves are permanently sterilized.[37] Countries do not tend to stay forever in balance-of-payments surplus or deficit. A country that accumulated reserves while a sink will have the ability to run deficits for a longer period if its payments position reverses. Thus the initial expansion of international liquidity may generate more expansionary policies by some countries at a latter stage.

These second-stage effects would bring the long-run effects of international liquidity expansion closer to the predictions of the international reserve monetarists, but the lags involved would be both much longer and more variable than in the case of national economy responses to money supply changes. Indeed, these lags might often be measured in decades, rather than years.

There is also reason to believe that a considerable portion of the

---

[37] This has been emphasized by Harry G. Johnson, "International Liquidity and Balance of Payments: Comment," in *International Reserves*, pp. 147–51, and Jürg Niehans, "The Need for Reserves of a Single Country," in *International Reserves*, pp. 49–85.

reserves that initially flow into reserve sinks may be permanently sterilized. There is likely to be a dependence effect in operation. As Fritz Machlup has argued, reserve accumulations are likely to ratchet up the minimum reserve levels with which financial authorities feel comfortable.[38] Because of the public choice considerations discussed above, such bureaucratic objectives may often have a major impact on the ultimate decisions. This is illustrated in figure 2. The increase in reserves from, say, a to b would shift the DD curve to the right by some fraction of this amount. To the extent that such an effect does operate, after a country moved into deficit its authorities would begin to implement adjustment policies at a higher level of reserves than if the additional accumulation had not occurred. To date, there has been no formal empirical study of the magnitudes of such dependence effects, but casual empiricism suggests that they might be quite

[38] Fritz Machlup, "The Need for Monetary Reserves," Banca Nazionale del Lavoro *Quarterly Review*, no. 78 (September 1966), pp. 175–222.

FIGURE 2
RATCHET EFFECTS IN THE DEMAND FOR RESERVES

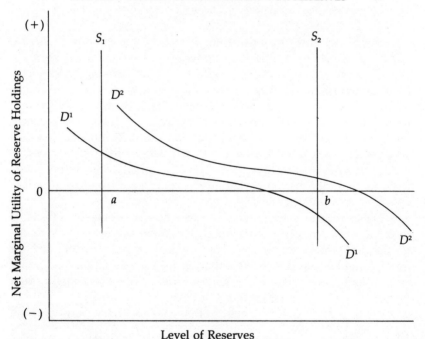

Level of Reserves

NOTE: See notes to figure 1.

large.[39] Japan's balance-of-payments experience over the past decades, for example, is quite consistent with the hypothesis of a sizable dependence effect. So is the relatively modest amount of dollars sold off by the European countries after floating exchange rates were adopted in 1973. (This will be discussed below.) To the extent that such ratchet or dependence effects operate, some, and perhaps a large portion, of the flow of reserves into reserve sinks would be permanently rather than only temporarily sterilized.[40]

Of course, discussions of possible slippages between reserve changes and national spending do not guarantee that important empirical regularities may not be found that can be useful for aggregate control. When looking at the behavior of particular economic entities, one could easily convince oneself that there would be little connection between the supply of money and private economic spending. Yet we know from extensive empirical testing that although there is variability in the exact effects of changes in monetary aggregates on private spending, the relationships are not usually sufficiently strong to make the control of monetary aggregates an important aspect of macroeconomic policies. (This proposition would be accepted by most nonmonetarists as well as monetarists, although not in a form that advocated fixed monetary growth rules.)

Might not the same apply with respect to international reserve monetarism? I doubt that this is the case. There are, of course, some empirical regularities with respect to studies of the demand for international reserves that help explain why some countries hold higher levels of reserves than others. Finding statistical significance in such studies is quite consistent with there being enormous variability in aggregate relationships. Several studies recently have looked at aggregate relationships between changes in international reserve totals and world inflation.[41]

The examination of the strong divergence between the aggregate and country-to-country results for the 1970–1972 period discussed

---

[39] Although they did not directly test the Machlup ratchet effect, Bilson and Frenkel in "Dynamic Adjustment and the Demand for International Reserves" tested a related hypothesis, which could be derived from the Machlup approach. They found that industrial countries tend to adjust more rapidly to an even demand for reserves than to an excess supply. Bilson and Frenkel caution that they lacked sufficient observations of cases of excess supply to have great confidence in their results; the results are nevertheless suggestive, especially when combined with the similar findings of Michael Michaely in *Balance-of-Payments Adjustment Policies: Japan, Germany, and the Netherlands*, National Bureau of Economic Research Occasional Paper No. 106 (New York: National Bureau of Economic Research, 1968).

[40] For further analysis on this point, see Sweeney and Willett, "Eurodollars, Petrodollars, and World Liquidity," pp. 277–310.

[41] See, for example, Heller, "International Reserves and Worldwide Inflation"; Heller and Khan, "The Demand for International Reserves"; Michael K. Keran, "Towards an

above may make one suspicious, however, about the extent to which such statistical analysis of aggregated national data has really picked up economically meaningful causal relationships of great strength. Particularly with equations with a large number of lags, it is often possible ex post to fit regressions that have strong statistical properties, but are of little economic significance or use in forecasting future relationships.[42]

In my judgment, support from much more detailed and disaggregated empirical studies would be required before acceptance of any strong form of the international reserve monetarism hypothesis is justified.

An initial look at the developments immediately following the adoption of generalized floating does not offer much support for strong forms of the international reserve monetarism view. From this perspective, the limited magnitude of the runoff of European reserves in 1973 and 1974 must be considered surprisingly small.

Reserve Runoffs after the Adoption of Floating Rates

As is indicated in table 4, the Western European countries did take advantage of the adoption of floating exchange rates in 1973 to sell off over $5 billion worth of international reserves in aggregate during 1973 and 1974. From a monthly peak of $47.5 billion in October 1973, official dollar holdings declined to a low of $42.3 billion in August 1974.

By the end of 1974, however, aggregate European reserve holdings were rising again. The maximum runoff of $5.2 billion in official dollar holdings for Western Europe during 1973 and 1974 was only about 15 percent of the more than $40 billion increase in reserves from the beginning of 1970. Of course, there would have been a normal increase in the demand for reserves over this period. The value of Western Europe's international trade grew by approximately 86 percent from 1970 through 1973. Assuming that the Western European reserve holdings were in equilibrium at the beginning of 1970 and assuming a one-for-one relation between the value of trade and

Explanation of Simultaneous Inflation-Recession," San Francisco Federal Reserve Bank *Business Review* (Spring 1975), pp. 18–30; and D. I. Meiselman, "Worldwide Inflation: A Monetarist View," in Meiselman and Laffer, *Worldwide Inflation*, pp. 69–112.

[42] For further discussion of questions on the economic significance of these aggregate studies, see Sweeney and Willett, "Eurodollars, Petrodollars, and World Liquidity," pp. 277–310. See also, however, the more recent study by H. Robert Heller, "Further Evidence on the Relationship between International Reserves and World Inflation" (mimeographed, International Monetary Fund, 1977), which meets some, although in my judgment not all, of the criticisms and questions raised by Sweeney and Willett.

TABLE 4

U.S. LIABILITIES TO OFFICIAL FOREIGN INSTITUTIONS, 1970–1975
(billions of dollars, amounts outstanding)

Date	Total	Western Europe[a]
1975 December	80.6	45.7
November	80.2	45.1
October	80.7	45.3
September	78.8	45.8
August	79.9	44.3
July	80.3	44.5
June	80.8	45.5
May	80.0	45.5
April	79.3	45.2
March	79.3	45.9
February	78.7	44.8
January	76.0	43.3
1974 December	76.6	44.2
November	75.2	43.2
October	73.8	43.0
September	72.7	42.7
August	71.1	42.3
July	71.1	43.0
June	70.0	43.2
May	68.2	42.9
April	67.2	42.6
March	65.5	42.8
February	64.1	42.4
January	63.9	43.3
1973 December	66.9	45.7
November	67.4	46.0
October	69.7	47.5
September	69.8	47.1
August	70.5	47.3
July	71.0	47.1
June	70.7	47.0
May	70.9	46.6
April	70.1	45.6
March	71.3	45.2
February	68.5	40.8
January	60.8	34.1
1972 December	61.5	34.2
1971 January	20.5	13.7
1970 January	12.7	6.3

[a] Includes Bank of International Settlements and European Fund.

SOURCE: U.S. Department of the Treasury, *Treasury Bulletin*, table IFS–3, various issues.

the demand for reserves, this would have accounted for an $11.8 billion increase in the demand for reserves.[43] The huge growth in the value of international trade in 1974 because of the oil price increases would have accounted for a further increase of $15.1 billion. This crudely adjusted calculation of the excess supply of reserves still shows that over $14 billion of the initial reserve imbalance was not reversed.

Of course, several other important factors were also at work. Increased uncertainty and expected variability of balance-of-payments positions would further increase the demand for international reserves. On the other hand, by reducing the costs of adjustment for many countries, the adoption of floating exchange rates would be expected both to reduce the demand for international reserves and to reduce the costs of selling off an excess supply of reserves.[44] Coun-

---

[43] This assumption of a one-to-one relationship is likely to bias upward the calculation, as optimal inventory approaches to both the demand for money and the demand for international reserves suggest that there should be economies of scale in reserve demands with respect to an increase in the volume of transactions. Under pegged exchange rates, the value of the elasticity of the demand for reserves with respect to imports appears typically to have been between 0.8 and 1.0. See, for example, Polak, "Money: National and International," pp. 510–20, and Heller and Khan, "The Demand for International Reserves," pp. 623–49. Some lower estimates have recently been made by Frenkel, however. See Frenkel, "International Reserves, Pegged Exchange Rates, and Managed Floating"; Frenkel, "International Reserves under Pegged Exchange Rates and Managed Float"; Bilson and Frenkel, "Dynamic Adjustment and the Demand for International Reserves," and Frenkel and Jovanovic, "Optimal International Reserves."

[44] It would theoretically be possible for the adoption of managed floating to increase the demand for international reserves, if private speculation behaved in a sufficiently perverse manner. This possibility was raised by Roy Harrod in *Reforming the World's Money* (London: Macmillan, 1965), and was analyzed in more detail by John Williamson in "Exchange Rate Flexibility and Reserve Use," *Scandinavian Journal of Economics*, vol. 78, no. 2 (1976), pp. 327–39. In practice, however, private speculation appears to have predominantly stabilizing, rather than destabilizing, effects. See, for example, Willett, *Floating Exchange Rates*, chap. 2; Dennis Logue, Richard Sweeney, and Thomas D. Willett, "The Speculative Behavior of Exchange Rates during the Current Float," *Journal of Business Research*, vol. 6, no. 2 (May 1978), pp. 159–74; and the references cited in these works. Although there is still very heavy intervention, the net effect of adopting the floating rates appears to have been a reduction in the demand for international reserves, ceteris paribus. See, for example, Heller and Khan, "Demand for International Reserves," pp. 623–49.

The rationale, of course, is that the higher cost of adjustment that can be avoided or postponed through the use of reserves, the higher the demand for reserves. The analysis assumes that for many countries exchange-rate changes will be a less costly method of adjustment than demand management. As is emphasized in the theory of optimum currency areas (see Tower and Willett, "Theory of Optimum Currency Areas," and references cited there), this will not be true for all countries, especially not for small, open ones; nevertheless, the adoption of managed flexible rates gives countries greater freedom to use exchange-rate changes, if they so desire, without prohibiting the use of demand management. The cost of adjustment for some countries would thus be lowered, while for others it would be unaffected. In aggregate, this

tries would no longer have to adopt more inflationary domestic policies in order to run down reserves, as was required under pegged exchange rates. In terms of figure 1, the adoption of floating rates would both shift the *DD* schedule to the left and collapse the costs of adjustment lines in toward the horizontal axis. On both grounds, one would expect a larger and more rapid sell-off of reserves than would occur under pegged exchange rates.[45]

The Increased Market Value of Gold. Over this period, a further huge increase in potential international liquidity had been generated by the rise in gold prices associated with the breakdown of the Bretton Woods exchange-rate arrangements. Indeed, if official gold stocks were valued at private market rather than official prices, the increase in official international liquidity from this source was of even greater magnitude than the increase in official foreign exchange holdings resulting from the U.S. payments deficit. National gold stocks, with an official value of $43.7 billion, were worth more than three times that amount if valued at market prices.[46]

This increase in potential international liquidity did not generate the same direct pressures for monetary expansion as were caused by the U.S. payments imbalances. Those imbalances represented the appreciation of the value of already-held assets. This appreciation could have an expansionary wealth effect on the spending of private gold holders, but would cause no direct inflationary pressures that required monetary sterilization to offset them. Thus the appreciation of gold did not directly generate monetary expansion, even in small countries with limited ability to sterilize reserve inflows.

The increased value of national gold stocks could facilitate increased spending, however. Even with the abandonment of official gold transactions among monetary authorities, official gold stocks could be sold to the private market. Such sales would help to finance government budget deficits, as well as balance-of-payments deficits when sales were to foreigners. The increased market value of gold

---

would unambiguously lead to a decline in the aggregate demand for reserves, with the magnitude depending in part on optimum currency area considerations. In my own judgment, the adoption of flexible exchange rates reduced the cost of adjustment for most of the European countries.

[45] Although aggregate foreign dollar holdings could be reduced only through a balance-of-payments surplus by the United States or through the reversal of dollar creation in offshore markets, such as the Eurodollar market, official dollar holdings of the European countries could be reduced through sales either to the private market or to other countries, such as the members of OPEC.

[46] See David Fand, "World Reserves and World Inflation," Banca Nazionale del Lavoro *Quarterly Review*, no. 115 (December 1975), p. 150.

holdings could also be used, and sometimes was used, as collateral for balance-of-payments loans from other financial authorities.[47]

This huge increase in the potential market value of gold holdings further undercut the meaningfulness of the official international reserve aggregates. It should have also increased the desires of countries to sell off official dollar holdings along international monetarist lines. Given the strong efforts being made to demonetize gold officially and the sharp divergence between the official and market prices of gold, actual official transactions in gold virtually came to a halt for several years. This would not eliminate the potential expansionary effects of the gold price increases, however. Many countries appeared to have a strong preference for maintaining their gold holdings, but thought of them as a last line of defense.

An increase in the value of this last line of defense would thus increase total effective liquidity and shift the DD curve in figure 1 to the right. Under these assumptions, the excess supply of international liquidity that would be sold off would be foreign exchange holdings. Of course, what would be important here is how officials viewed their effective liquidity position, not the extent to which they followed France's example and marked up the value of their gold stocks in their own financial accounts.[48]

In light of all of these developments, the rather limited sell-off of international reserves during 1973 and 1974 would have to seem rather surprising from the standpoint of a strong international reserve monetarism perspective.

Transitional Considerations. Of course, the oil shock and resulting increases in the demand for international reserves did limit the period over which there should have been strong pressures to sell off excess reserves. Even with the adoption of floating rates, one would not expect all excess reserves to be sold off immediately. Floating rates greatly lowered the costs of adjusting an excess demand or supply of international reserves for many countries, but these costs were not completely eliminated. Under floating rates, such costs would be

---

[47] See, for example, ibid.

[48] The DD curve here refers to official reserves as measured by the International Monetary Fund, which still uses the official price of gold. If reserves were defined as including gold at a market or other higher price, as some countries have done in their national statistics, then this would be represented as a movement along the curve. One should arrive at the same description of behavior, whichever convention is adopted, except to the extent that balance-sheet considerations influence central bank or national behavior. Although such considerations may have contributed to the official aversion to revaluations because of the resulting accounting losses on reserves, the formal statistical treatment of the value of gold in national reserves would seem unlikely to have a major influence on behavior.

reflected in deviations of the exchange rate from levels desired on overall policy grounds. Often this goal could be approximated by the objective of avoiding large and rapid changes in exchange rates. The more rapidly reserves were sold off, the greater would be the appreciation of the exchange rate.

We live in a much less mercantilist world today than at many times in the past, but governments still tend to be sensitive to taking policy measures that reduce the competitiveness of their trade positions. This sensitivity would limit the rate at which financial authorities would want to sell off an excess supply of reserves.

Thus, even though authorities had a much less expensive method of running down excess reserves, they would not want to sell off all of these reserves immediately. The rate at which excess reserves tended to be sold off would be less—

- the less was the total excess surplus of reserves;
- the less the authorities were concerned by the misallocation of resources resulting from above-optimal reserve holdings;
- the more governments were concerned with export and import competing producer interests relative to those of the users of imports;
- the greater was their concern about exchange-rate variations; and
- the less were market pressures generating a tendency toward balance-of-payments deficit or exchange-rate depreciation in the absence of official actions.

The aggregate rate at which reserves were sold off would also be less, the more highly concentrated in a few countries was the bulk of total excess reserves. As is indicated in table 5, most countries shared in the reserve increase of 1970–1972, but a few of the major industrial countries accounted for a significant portion of the total.

For such reasons it is quite likely that the total amount of excess supplies of international reserves was not worked off in 1973 and 1974. The oil price increases had a two-sided effect, however. They greatly increased uncertainty and hence the precautionary demand for international reserves, but the huge increase in oil import payments offered a means of running down excess reserve holdings with little adjustment costs. Thus although the oil shock reduced the level of excess reserves it also reduced the cost of selling off that portion of reserves that was still in excess.

The available evidence is not conclusive, but the reversal toward increased demands for reserves during 1974 seems quite consistent with the view that the supply-determined international liquidity explosion of 1970–1972 ratcheted up the minimum levels of reserve positions with which many monetary authorities felt comfortable.

International Liquidity Implications of the Oil Shock

The extent to which there was such an increase in the demand for reserves had important implications for the appropriate international liquidity response to the oil shock. It was clear that for many years a number of the OPEC countries would be earning revenues greatly in excess of their international expenditures, and that there would be only limited scope for exchange-rate adjustments to reduce this imbalance for a number of years. Likewise, it was unreasonable to expect that a sizable portion of their resulting net foreign investment would not go into the types of liquid assets traditionally recorded as international reserves. As a consequence, unless the international payments system broke down, these countries would have to acquire large holdings of international reserves. Although some initial projections greatly overstated the likely magnitude of these accumulations, even the more "optimistic" projections foresaw accumulations on the order of $200 billion over the rest of the 1970s.[49]

Again, this was a situation in which the behavior of reserve aggregates was likely to give a misleading picture of the overall degree of reserve stringency in the world economy. Clearly, such a large redistribution of reserves would not be manageable within the context of only modest aggregate reserve growth without placing severe deflationary pressures on many oil-importing countries. Nor was it clear to what extent the pressures of reserve stringency would result in deflationary domestic economic policies or in beggar-thy-neighbor trade and exchange-rate policies.

Views on the appropriate response for international liquidity aggregates varied widely. To the extent that there were substantial excess reserves still in the system, the demands in the oil-exporting countries would allow these reserves to be used up without the need for a corresponding growth in reserve totals. On the other hand, if the past reserve increases had generated their own demand to a large extent, through ratchet effects, or if there was little scope to run down these excess reserves without substantial adjustment costs, a substantial increase in international liquidity would be required if severe deflationary pressures on a number of countries were to be avoided.

[49] For a discussion of, and for references on, this issue, see Thomas D. Willett, *The Oil Transfer Problem and International Economic Stability*, Princeton Essays in International Finance, no. 113 (Princeton, N.J.: International Finance Section, Princeton University, 1975).

Such uncertainties were compounded by lack of knowledge about the quantitative effects of the other factors discussed above, the adoption of greater exchange-rate flexibility and the gold price increases, on reducing the demand for currency reserves, and the effects of the oil-induced international financial uncertainties on increasing the demand. Given the lack of previous experience with such developments, one had little basis on which to judge, much less precisely estimate, the magnitude of such effects.[50]

It is hard to know what the official response would have been had we had true international control over international reserve aggregates. My guess is that we may have been fortunate that we did not have such control. I doubt that any IMF body or group of leading finance ministry officials would have voted to create nearly as much international liquidity as was generated by decentralized decisions during the following years. However, on balance, I am skeptical that substantially too much aggregate international liquidity was generated.[51] Given the widespread fears at the time that the oil situation would lead to a breakdown in international cooperation and a return to the beggar-thy-neighbor scramble of the 1930s, a strong case can be made that it was much better to err on the side of allowing too much reserve creation rather than too little. With flexible exchange rates, countries had a good deal of scope to shield themselves from the effects of excessive international liquidity creation.

Although many countries suffered from high rates of inflation over this period, this was due much more to the direct effects of the oil price increases and macroeconomic policy choices, made primarily on domestic grounds, than to the pressures generated by the operation of the international monetary system.[52] Whether there should have been more or less monetary accommodation to the oil shocks remains a controversial question. While some have argued that the following global recession was unnecessarily severe because national governments did not fully understand the direct deflationary effects

---

[50] For an interesting effort in this direction, however, see John H. Makin, "Reserve Adequacy Before and After Limited Floating," *Journal of Economics and Business*, vol. 30, no. 1 (Fall 1977), pp. 8–14. See also the later work by Heller and Khan, "Demand for International Reserves," pp. 623–49.

[51] In a similar vein, Robert Triffin has argued that "the slowness of the international decision-making process—even under the weighted-voting *majority* procedures of the IMF as opposed to the usual *unanimity* rule—might have seriously impeded the prompt recycling of OPEC surpluses if they had been channeled into SDRs or similar reserve holdings with the IMF rather than into dollars and Eurodollars." Triffin, *Gold and the Dollar Crisis*, Princeton Essays in International Finance, no. 132 (Princeton, N.J.: International Finance Section, Princeton University, 1978), p. 12.

[52] Of these factors, domestic macroeconomic policy choices caused by far the greatest proportion of inflation in most countries.

TABLE 5

DISTRIBUTION OF RESERVES, END OF YEARS 1950, 1960, AND 1970–1977[1]

Countries	1950	1960	1970	1971	1972	1973	1974	1975	1976	1977
Industrial countries										
Austria	—	0.7	1.8	2.2	2.5	2.4	2.8	3.8	3.8	3.5
Belgium-Luxembourg	0.8	1.5	2.8	3.2	3.6	4.2	4.4	5.0	4.5	4.7
Canada	1.8	2.0	4.7	5.3	5.6	4.8	4.8	4.5	5.0	3.8
Denmark	0.1	0.3	0.5	0.7	0.8	1.1	0.8	0.7	0.8	1.4
France	0.8	2.3	5.0	7.6	9.2	7.4	7.2	10.8	8.4	8.4
Germany, Federal Republic of	0.2	7.0	13.6	17.2	21.9	27.5	26.5	26.5	30.0	32.7
Italy	0.7	3.3	5.4	6.3	5.6	5.3	5.7	4.1	5.7	9.6
Japan	0.6	1.9	4.8	14.1	16.9	10.2	11.0	10.9	14.3	19.1
Netherlands	0.5	1.9	3.2	3.5	4.4	5.4	5.7	6.1	6.4	6.6
Norway	0.1	0.3	0.8	1.1	1.2	1.3	1.6	1.9	1.9	1.8
Sweden	0.3	0.5	0.8	1.0	1.5	2.1	1.4	2.6	2.1	3.0
Switzerland	1.6	2.3	5.1	6.4	7.0	7.1	7.4	8.9	11.2	11.4
United Kingdom	4.8	5.1	2.8	8.1	5.2	5.4	5.7	4.7	3.6	17.3
United States	24.3	19.4	14.5	12.1	12.1	11.9	13.1	13.6	15.8	16.0
Total, industrial countries	36.8	48.5	65.8	88.8	97.5	96.0	97.9	104.1	113.5	139.4
Primary producing countries										
More developed countries										
Other European countries[2]	1.5	2.3	5.6	8.0	11.7	13.4	12.4	11.1	11.8	12.9
Australia, New Zealand, South Africa	2.0	1.3	3.0	4.2	7.6	6.5	5.0	4.2	4.0	3.0
Subtotal	3.5	3.6	8.5	12.1	19.4	19.9	17.3	15.3	15.8	15.9

Less developed countries										
Major oil-exporting countries[3]	1.3	2.3	5.0	7.8	10.0	12.0	38.4	48.3	56.1	62.1
Other less developed countries										
Other Western Hemisphere[4]	2.4	2.2	4.5	4.5	7.5	10.0	9.7	8.6	13.1	16.7
Other Middle East[5]	1.1	0.7	1.6	2.0	2.7	3.6	3.9	4.4	5.0	6.3
Other Asia[6]	3.7	2.7	5.8	6.3	7.8	8.8	10.5	11.3	16.3	19.3
Other Africa[7]	0.5	0.9	2.0	1.7	1.9	2.2	2.4	2.4	2.6	3.0
Subtotal, other less developed countries	7.7	6.6	13.9	14.5	19.9	24.6	26.5	26.7	36.9	45.4
Subtotal, less developed countries[8]	9.9	9.0	18.9	22.3	29.9	36.6	64.9	75.0	93.1	107.5
Total, primary producing countries	13.4	12.6	27.4	34.4	49.3	56.5	82.2	90.3	108.9	123.4
Total	50.2	61.2	93.2	123.2	146.8	152.6	180.2	194.5	222.4	262.8

[1] In billions of SDRs. Official reserves of fund members except Romania, plus the Netherlands Antilles and Switzerland. In addition to the holdings covered in *International Financial Statistics (IFS)* (Washington, D.C.: International Monetary Fund), the figures for 1973 include official French claims on the European Monetary Cooperation Fund; those for 1950 and 1960 include amounts incorporated in published U.K. reserves in 1966 and 1967 from proceeds of liquidation of the U.K. official portfolio of dollar securities. For a number of countries (beginning in 1974, United States; in 1975, France; in 1976, Italy, Mexico, and Jordan; and in 1977, Australia, Costa Rica, Cameroon, Central African Empire, Chad, People's Republic of the Congo, and Gabon) stock reserve figures may differ from those published in national sources because of differences in valuation of gold, which in the *IFS* is valued at 35 SDRs per ounce. Totals may not add to figures shown because of rounding and because some totals include unpublished data for component areas.

[2] Finland, Greece, Iceland, Ireland, Malta, Portugal, Spain, Turkey, and Yugoslavia.

[3] Algeria, Indonesia, Iran, Iraq, Kuwait, Libya, Nigeria, Saudi Arabia, Venezuela, and, beginning in 1970, Oman and Qatar, and in 1973, the United Arab Emirates.

[4] Argentina, Bolivia, Brazil, Central America, Chile, Colombia, the Dominican Republic, Ecuador, Guyana, Haiti, Jamaica, Mexico, Panama, Paraguay, Peru, Suriname, Trinidad and Tobago, Uruguay, and, beginning in 1970, the Bahamas, Barbados, and the Netherlands Antilles.

[5] Cyprus, Egypt, Israel, Jordan, Lebanon, the Syrian Arab Republic, and, beginning in 1970, the People's Democratic Republic of Yemen and Bahrain, and in 1973, the Yemen Arab Republic.

[6] Afghanistan, Burma, the Republic of China, India, Korea, Malaysia, Nepal, Pakistan, the Philippines, Singapore, Sri Lanka, Thailand, Vietnam, and, beginning in 1970, Fiji, Lao People's Democratic Republic, and Western Samoa; in 1972, Bangladesh; and in 1973, Papua New Guinea.

[7] African fund members other than Algeria, Libya, Nigeria, and South Africa.

[8] Includes residual.

SOURCE: International Monetary Fund, *Annual Report*, 1978, p. 51.

of the oil price increases and the collective limits on each country's individual ability to export its way out of recession, others believe that there was excessive monetary accommodation that further fueled the fires of worldwide inflation.

These disagreements rest on both normative and positive issues and are unlikely ever to be fully resolved. Inflation was clearly excessive in the sense that it was higher than most people would have liked. However, given the worsened short-run relationships between inflation and output caused by the oil price increase, the question of whether monetary accommodation was itself excessive is in my judgment an open one. My own normative view would be that while monetary accommodation during the last decade has generally been excessive, this may well not have been the case in the oil shock episode.

What is relevant for this study, however, is not the overall issue of the appropriate degree of monetary accommodation, but the appropriateness of international liquidity developments. Given the serious danger of widespread beggar-thy-neighbor trade and exchange-rate policies pointed out above, one can consistently argue that in general there has been a political bias toward excessive national monetary accommodation, but that the oil shock was a particular type of episode in which considerable international reserve ease still made sense.[53]

Criteria for Evaluating Excessive International Liquidity Creation

Because of their ability to create in effect international currency reserves by borrowing from private international financial markets, many countries were able to run more expansionary policies than would have otherwise been the case. As a result, the average level of world inflation was increased.

Some commentators took this as direct evidence that too much international liquidity was created. According to this view, international financial arrangements are too permissive if they allow countries to follow more inflationary pressures than the external observer thinks is appropriate. The international monetary system is viewed as a mechanism for constraining the options of national governments in order to secure policies more in line with those that the observer desires. From the perspective of many who are greatly concerned

[53] For further discussion of the political economy of monetary accommodation, see Leroy Laney and Thomas D. Willett, "United States Monetary Policy and the Political Business Cycle," Claremont Working Papers (Claremont, Calif.: Claremont Graduate School, 1980), and references cited there.

about inflation, international monetary arrangements are judged deficient if they allow such "excessively" inflationary pressures to be undertaken. Indeed, although such reasoning is seldom fully spelled out, I believe that this is one of the most important motivations for charges that the current arrangements for the provisions of international liquidity are seriously deficient.

In my judgment, however, this is not a satisfactory criterion for evaluating the operation of the international liquidity mechanism or, indeed, of the international monetary system in general. In the first place, reasonable people may have different views about how much inflation is "excessive" under various circumstances. Thus it is certainly not an unambiguous standard.

Given divergencies of view about what is correct, it would seem that the ideal international monetary mechanism would be one that gave each country the greatest ability to make its own decisions, subject to limits on the adverse effects such decisions might have on other countries. In other words, a liberal approach to the design of the international monetary system would attempt to minimize the external constraints placed on domestic economic policy making, the rationale for constraints being the protection of other countries from the export of serious economic instabilities or beggar-thy-neighbor policies.

From this perspective, the criterion for judging the operation of the international liquidity mechanism is to what extent liquidity creation that improved the economic position of some countries, as viewed by their governments, may have had adverse effects on other countries. The availability of greater liquidity to deficit countries will of course allow them to engage in a greater export of inflation to other countries. Minimizing the export of inflationary pressures is not, however, a sufficient criterion for judging whether there has been excessive international liquidity creation. This is because the oil shock becomes much more complicated, especially when it is recognized that the response to greater reserve stringency may have been beggar-thy-neighbor trade and exchange-rate policies rather than less expansionary macroeconomic policies. Thus once one drops the assumptions of pegged exchange rates with liberal trade policies, it is not always clear that placing greater adjustment pressures on a deficit country through greater reserve stringency will always reduce the export of negative externalities.

These considerations further illustrate the difficulties of judging the appropriateness of the operation of the international liquidity mechanism on the basis of the behavior of reserve totals or the rate of world inflation. The use of these criteria would have probably led to much less international liquidity creation over this period if such creation could have been centrally controlled. I do not wish to argue that there was an exactly optimal pattern and total amount of international liquidity creation over this period. On the contrary, I think there were a number of instances in which countries were able to finance large payments deficits for too long a period before they began to take serious adjustment actions. As will be argued below, however, the most effective way to reduce these instances of excessive payments deficits would have been through direct international surveillance of the international adjustment process.

Had the aggregate growth of international liquidity been considerably less, the odds that the often-predicted massive breakdown in international economic cooperation would have actually occurred would have been much greater. Although it was not fully planned by any means, the composite outcome of central and decentralized decisions was to err on the side of too much rather than too little international liquidity creation in response to the oil shock. In retrospect, this appears to me on balance to have been fortunate. I strongly agree with the judgment of Walter Salant, presented in an earlier context, that, "since the dangers of too high levels and too high growth [of international reserves] are much more easily offset by national policy than are those of too low levels and too low growth, it is better to overestimate than to underestimate needed levels of growth."[54]

In the context of the oil shock, one of the results of substantially less access to international liquidity would have been an increased likelihood of beggar-thy-neighbor trade policies. On the other hand, the effects of "excessive" access to international liquidity by deficit countries meant that these countries were able to prop up their exchange rates at artificial levels for too long. The effect of such actions on the stronger countries was that their exchange rates were depressed below equilibrium levels. In general, the currencies of the surplus countries did not appreciate as much as they would have in the absence of foreign official intervention. This did mean that the stronger countries faced higher import prices than otherwise, and thus would find it somewhat more difficult to achieve a given low inflation rate target. I doubt that the quantitative significance of this direct price transmission of inflationary pressures from deficit countries was extremely great, however. Furthermore, the stronger countries did have considerable scope for retaining control over the growth of their monetary aggregates.

---

[54] Salant, "Assessing the Need for World Reserves," p. 305.

It was when the surplus countries themselves intervened to hold down the appreciation of their currencies that they found direct international pressures for more rapid monetary expansion than they desired on domestic grounds. These imported inflationary pressures have in practice appeared to be of greater concern to the low-inflation countries such as Germany and Switzerland. The pressures stemmed not from excessive access to international liquidity by the deficit countries, but from official intervention based on perceptions (which may or may not have been well founded in reality) that destabilizing private speculation was causing excessive exchange-rate movements. There is little evidence that the high rate of international liquidity created over this period had more than relatively minor effects in terms of forcing individual countries to inflate more than their governments desired.[55]

There has been a long tradition of suspicion that governments will have biases toward overspending. This suspicion, for example, underlies arguments for the independence of central banks from governments. Recently there has been a growing body of analysis that has analyzed such questions more rigorously and similarly concludes that governments are likely to face incentives to follow more inflationary policies than would be desired by the majority of voters were they fully informed.[56]

This literature focuses on two topics: (1) tendencies toward excessive government expenditures and accompanying inflationary pressures that result from biases in the process of collective decision making; and (2) incentives to generate political business cycles and higher overall rates of inflation by exploiting voter myopia and differences between short-run and long-run relationships between inflation and unemployment. These considerations can provide a second-best argument for attempting to exert additional discipline on

---

[55] This is not to say that I do not believe that the average rate of world inflation has been too high over the past decade, not only in relation to an ideal, but also in relation to the hard policy choices which had to be made, given actual rather than ideal inflation-unemployment relationships.

[56] Major contributions and survey pieces on public choice analysis of macroeconomic policies and of the incentives to engage in political business cycles include: James M. Buchanan and Richard Wagner, *Democracy in Deficit* (New York: Academic Press, 1977); Burro S. Frey, "Politico-Economic Models and Cycles," *Journal of Public Economics*, vol. 9, no. 2 (April 1978), pp. 203–20; Fred Hirsch and John H. Goldthorpe, eds., *The Political Economy of Inflation* (Cambridge, Mass.: Harvard University Press, 1978); and W. D. Nordhaus, "The Political Business Cycle," *Review of Economic Studies*, vol. 42, no. 2 (April 1975), pp. 169–90. Extensive references to this rapidly growing literature are given in Frey, above; in Laney and Willett, "United States Monetary Policy and the Political Business Cycle"; and in Leroy Laney and Thomas D. Willett, *The Political Economy of Global Inflation: The Causes of Monetary Expansion in the Major Industrial Countries* (Washington, D.C.: American Enterprise Institute, forthcoming).

national governments through international monetary constraints. Such thinking has undoubtedly been behind the traditional arguments for the discipline of fixed exchange rates. In fact, however, the discipline implied by different international monetary systems is itself quite difficult to assess.[57]

On grounds of both reliability and democratic self-determination, the most appropriate response to perceived biases in the domestic decision-making process would be the implementation of constitutional measures to reduce these biases through domestic reforms. It is not reasonable to expect international monetary arrangements to serve this function. It is quite a sufficient set of tasks for the international monetary system to attempt to facilitate the greater degree of monetary independence (particularly for countries limiting capital inflows). Thus for concerns about inadequacy of private international liquidity one should look to the prevalence of capital controls, not to any particular relationships between private international liquidity holdings and the value of world trade.[58]

In recent years, the primary focus of concern has been the possibility of excessive private international liquidity, especially as a result of credit creation in the Eurocurrency markets. A frequently voiced concern is that the operation of the Eurocurrency markets has added greatly to the effects of monetary expansion by national authorities on the aggregate level of world spending, thus making a sizable unforeseen contribution to the acceleration of world inflation during the 1970s.

Such concerns have often been greatly exaggerated, however, often because of misleading comparisons between figures on the size of the Eurocurrency markets in relation to national money supplies. For example, newspaper stories periodically rediscover that some figures reported for the size of the Eurodollar market are several times the size of the U.S. money supply, narrowly defined. Likewise, people have frequently argued for financing international trade and in-

---

[57] See, for example, W. M. Corden, *Inflation, Exchange Rates, and the World Economy* (Chicago, Ill.: University of Chicago Press, 1977), and Thomas D. Willett and John Mullen, "The Effects of Alternative International Monetary Systems on Macro-Economic Discipline and the Political Business Cycle," Claremont Economic Papers (Claremont, Calif.: Claremont Graduate School, 1980).

[58] For further discussions on the concept of the adequacy of private international liquidity and how it is influenced by the adequacy of official international liquidity, see Thomas D. Willett, "The Adequacy of International Means of Payment," *Review of Economics and Statistics*, vol. 51, no. 3 (August 1969), pp. 373–74, and Fritz Machlup, "Further Reflections on the Demand for Foreign Reserves," in Fritz Machlup, ed., *International Payments, Debts, and Gold* (New York: Charles Scribner's Sons, 1964), pp. 260–76. See also Mahar and Porter, "International Reserves and Capital Mobility," pp. 205–19.

vestment while limiting the extent to which countries are subjected to the import of negative monetary and financial externalities from abroad.

Eurocurrency Markets and Private International Liquidity

Before turning to an analysis of current international liquidity policy issues, we will consider one more major area of international liquidity developments. This is the role of the private international financial markets, particularly the Eurocurrency markets. The use of these markets as a source for official borrowing has already been briefly touched upon above. In this section, the various major aspects of the international liquidity effects on the operation of the private international financial markets will be reviewed.

First, however, a brief digression on private international liquidity considerations is in order. A first point is that there is not a concept of the adequacy of private international liquidity analogous to that for official international liquidity. Private international liquidity is usually measured as the total of private holdings of liquid assets in foreign markets. In a free market, such holdings would be determined by the private calculation of economic advantage in financing trade and gaining maximum returns on investment. Liquidity would always be adequate by definition. An inadequacy of private international financial holdings would occur only as a result of restrictions on international capital movements. Such restrictions would tend to be the consequence of either official reserve inadequacy (for countries limiting capital outflows) or concern that a figure for the Eurocurrency markets should be added into estimates of the aggregate world money supply. Such analysis often fails to recognize that most of the approximately $800 billion of the gross figures for the size of the Eurocurrency markets is already covered in national monetary statistics. Furthermore, only a very small portion of Eurocurrency market assets have the same degree of liquidity as the funds included in even the broadly defined measures of national money supplies, such as M_2 and M_3.[59] The substantial majority of the financial assets in the Eu-

---

[59] For further discussion of these points, see Sweeney and Willett, "Eurodollars, Petrodollars, and World Liquidity," pp. 277–310; Helmut W. Mayer, "The BIS Concept of the Eurocurrency Market," *Euromoney* (May 1976), pp. 60–66; Morgan Guaranty Trust, "The Eurocurrency Market," *World Financial Markets* (January 1979), pp. 9–14; and Adrian W. Throop, "Eurobanking and World Inflation," *Voice of the Federal Reserve Bank of Dallas* (August 1979), pp. 8–23. For recent general discussion of the Eurocurrency markets, and for references to the extensive literature in this area, see Andrew D. Crockett, "The Eurocurrency Market: An Attempt to Clarify Some Basic Issues," *IMF Staff Papers*, vol. 23, no. 2 (Washington, D.C.: International Monetary Fund, 1976), pp. 375–86; Gunter Dufey and Ian H. Giddy, *The International Money Market* (Englewood

rocurrency markets would conventionally be called credit, rather than money.

It is true that the Eurocurrency markets do have an effect on global monetary conditions, but the quantitative magnitude is actually relatively small. While there is some effective money and credit creation resulting from the operation of these markets, it is highly unlikely that this has been a major source of global inflationary pressures. From the standpoint of national financial authorities, the expansion of the Eurocurrency markets could best be thought of as having caused, ceteris paribus, a slight increase in the velocity of the money supplies as traditionally measured.[60]

The other major aspect of the Eurocurrency markets and national monetary control is really a question of international capital mobility per se.[61] National monetary authorities have often complained that the rate of capital flow into or out of the Eurocurrency markets is complicating or undercutting the operation of domestic monetary policy. Such authorities have often advocated such measures as requiring reserve requirements on Eurocurrency holdings as methods of reducing such problems.[62]

The issue here is not really one of the Eurocurrency markets, however, but of international capital mobility in general. At present the Eurocurrency markets happen to be the least-cost conduit for a substantial portion of international liquid-capital flows. This does not mean, however, that if the Eurocurrency markets were regulated out of existence, international capital mobility would decline to a corre-

---

Cliffs, N.J.: Prentice-Hall, 1978); Jane S. Little, "Liquidity Creation by Euro-banks: 1973–1978," *New England Economic Review* (January/February 1979), pp. 62–72; Ronald I. McKinnon, "Review of Floating Exchange Rates and International Monetary Reform," *Journal of Economic Literature*, vol. 16, no. 4 (December 1978), pp. 1469–71; Jürg Niehans and John Hewson, "The Eurocurrency Market and Monetary Theory," *Journal of Money, Credit, and Banking*, vol. 8, no. 1 (February 1976), pp. 1–29; Carl Stem, Dennis Logue, and John Makin, eds., *Eurocurrencies and the International Monetary System* (Washington, D.C.: American Enterprise Institute, 1976); and Manfred Willms, "Money Creation in the Eurocurrency Market," *Weltwirtschaftliches Archiv*, Heft 2 (1976), pp. 201–30.
[60] For further discussion on this point, see Willett, "Eurocurrency Market, Exchange-Rate Systems, and National Financial Policies."
[61] There is also an issue that lies beyond the scope of this study: the supervision of the safety of lending in the international financial markets and provisions for avoiding a credit collapse in the face of defaults or liquidity squeezes. In recent years, there has been a considerable advance in the understandings among major central banks regarding divisions of lender-of-last-resort responsibilities for international banking activities. For recent discussions of such international credit issues, see J. Carter Murphy, *The International Monetary System* (Washington, D.C.: American Enterprise Institute, 1979), and Robert L. Sammons, "International Debt: Its Growth and Significance" (Study prepared for the Special Study on Economic Change of the Joint Economic Committee, U.S. Congress, 1979).
[62] See, for example, Guido Carli et al., "A Debate on the Eurodollar Market," *Quaderni di Ricerche*, Ente per gli studi monetari, bancari e finanziari "Luigi Einaudi," no. 11

sponding degree. On the contrary, the majority of transactions that now go through the Eurocurrency markets would merely be diverted to other channels. One would expect some decline in international capital mobility, as a preferred method was eliminated for many investors and borrowers, but the overall effects on the international mobility of capital would be likely to be relatively marginal. Our world economy is far from completely integrated; as was noted earlier, empirical studies indicate that even under pegged exchange rates many countries had considerably more ability to control their domestic monetary conditions in the short run than was often implied by officials. International capital mobility is sufficiently high, however, that its effects must be taken into account in implementing domestic monetary policies.[63]

To preserve a high degree of monetary independence, then, most countries must either accept exchange-rate variability or adopt comprehensive capital controls. There are, of course, many disadvantages to the latter course, but it is what is required if a country wants a great deal of monetary independence and is not willing to accept substantial exchange-rate variability. Given the degree of economic interdependence among nations, it is a vain hope that this dilemma could be substantially reduced by international regulation and control of the Eurocurrency markets.

Now let us return to questions of the control of official international liquidity.

Official Reserve Holdings in the Eurocurrency Markets

The Eurocurrency markets have been increasingly important both as a location for international reserve holdings and as a source of borrowing for deficit countries through which international reserves are

---

(1972); R. Ossola, "Central Bank Intervention and Eurocurrency Markets," Banca Nazionale del Lavoro *Quarterly Review*, no. 104 (March 1973), pp. 29–45; and Paola Savona, "Controlling the Euromarkets," Banca Nazionale del Lavoro *Quarterly Review*, no. 109 (June 1974), pp. 167, 174. For a recent, well-balanced analysis of the effects of the Eurocurrency markets, and for a proposal for establishing a uniform minimum reserve requirement for all Eurocurrencies, see Henry C. Wallich, "Statement on the Eurocurrency Markets," and accompanying "Discussion Paper Concerning Reserve Requirements on Eurocurrency Deposits" by the Federal Reserve Board staff (presented to the Subcommittee on International Trade, Investment, and Monetary Policy of the Committee on Banking, Finance, and Urban Affairs, U.S. House of Representatives, U.S. Congress, July 12, 1979).

[63] For discussions on, and for references to the literature on, the effects of international capital mobility on the effectiveness of monetary and fiscal policy under pegged and flexible exchange rates, see Richard N. Cooper, "Monetary Theory and Policy in an Open Economy," *Scandinavian Journal of Economics*, vol. 78, no. 2 (1976), pp. 146–65; and Willett, "Eurocurrency Market, Exchange-Rate Systems, and National Financial Policies."

generated. The earliest development of quantitative significance began occurring in the 1960s, as central banks began to place a portion of their dollar accumulation in the Eurocurrency markets rather than holding it exclusively in bank deposits and Treasury securities in the United States. This broke the link between U.S. official settlements deficits and the expansion of foreign official dollar holdings and also probably led to some direct reserve creation through the operation of the Eurocurrency markets.[64] Although they were unnoticed for a good while, the total magnitudes involved quickly grew. By 1970, identified official holdings of Eurocurrencies (almost all of which were in dollars) had become almost half as large as official dollar holdings—SDR 10.9 billion as contrasted with $23.8 billion (see table 6). Concern about the consequences of this development led to agreement among the major industrial countries in 1971 not to increase further their reserve holdings in the Eurocurrency markets.

The significance of this agreement was swamped by the huge U.S. payments deficits of 1970–1972. Eurocurrency reserve holdings by the nonindustrial countries did continue to grow rapidly over this period, however. As a result, total Eurocurrency reserve holdings almost doubled during 1972 (from SDR 11.6 billion to SDR 21.2 billion). At the same time, a significant movement to diversify Eurocurrency reserve holdings toward nondollar currencies began. These identified holdings rose from only SDR 0.4 billion in 1970 to SDR 3.2 billion in 1972. As is indicated in table 6, this trend has continued, with identified nondollar Eurocurrencies equaling SDR 12.3 billion of the total SDR 70.3 billion at the end of 1977.

After the adoption of floating exchange rates, Eurocurrency holdings became for several years a more important source of growth of international liquidity than direct claims on the United States. Not until 1976 did the latter show a larger increase. This shift toward a greater quantitative importance of the Eurocurrency markets in aggregate reserve increases reflected both the termination of the large supply-determined outpouring of dollars from the United States as a result of the adoption of floating rates and the huge increases in revenues of the oil-exporting countries, a large portion of which was deposited in the Eurocurrency markets. As is indicated in table 6, the Eurodollar holdings of the major oil-exporting countries rose from SDR 3.9 billion in 1972 to SDR 20.7 billion at the end of 1975.

---

[64] For further discussion, see John Hewson and Eisuke Sakakibara, "The Euro-Dollar Multiplier: A Portfolio Approach," *IMF Staff Papers*, vol. 21, no. 2 (Washington, D.C.: International Monetary Fund, 1974), pp. 307–28, and Helmut W. Mayer, *Some Theoretical Problems Relating to the Euro-Dollar Market*, Princeton Essays in International Finance, no. 79 (Princeton, N.J.: International Finance Section, Princeton University, 1970).

The relative magnitude of Eurocurrency and direct dollar reserve increases reversed again in 1976 and 1977, because of a combination of the decline in the OPEC surplus; the substantial rebuilding of weak reserve positions by several major industrial countries, particularly the United Kingdom; and the substantial weakening of the U.S. balance-of-payments and exchange-rate positions that resulted in substantial exchange-market intervention by a number of the major industrial countries. (This last episode will be discussed further below.)

Official Borrowing and "Uncontrolled" International Liquidity Creation

Over these initial years of the oil shock, the Eurocurrency markets also came into their own as a source of official borrowing to finance balance-of-payments deficits. The fact that many of the industrial nations as well as the upper-income less-developed countries financed their huge increase in oil payments with only relatively small reductions in their gross levels of reserves was due largely to a tremendous increase in official international borrowing from the private financial markets, particularly the United States and the Eurocurrency markets. This phenomenon had not been anticipated in many of the early discussions of the problems of recycling the oil surpluses. These initial discussions focused primarily on where the OPEC money would be put and what the resulting reshuffling generated by induced private capital flows would be. In practice, however, much of the ultimate matching of surplus and deficit financial positions came from direct borrowing activity by deficit countries.

The huge increase in oil surpluses of course created severe international financial strains, but the world avoided anything approaching the disasters that many leaders feared. The private financial markets proved to be quite resilient. This fact, combined with prudent financial behavior by the OPEC countries, official recycling through the International Monetary Fund, and official borrowing from the private financial markets, prevented the extreme financial and exchange-rate instability and trade warfare many had feared.

The majority of oil-importing countries responded in a much less mercantilist manner than many had anticipated. The initial fear was that the oil-importing countries individually would not be willing to bear the size of deficit collectively required by the OPEC surplus. The possibility of a resulting scramble for a total of individual balance of payments that was collectively unfeasible gave rise to the specter of a repeat of the destructive beggar-thy-neighbor scrambles for sur-

TABLE 6

Official Holdings of Foreign Exchange, by Type of Claim, End of Years 1970–1977[a]
(billions of SDRs)

	1970	1971	1972	1973	1974	1975	1976	1977
Official claims on United States[b]	23.8	46.6	56.7	55.4	62.8	68.9	79.2	103.8
Official sterling claims on United Kingdom	5.7	7.3	8.1	6.5	8.3	6.4	3.2	3.3
Official deutsche mark claims on Fed. Rep. of Germany	1.3	1.0	1.4	2.2	2.4	2.5	4.3	5.7
Official French franc claims on France	0.6	0.8	1.0	1.2	1.1	1.1	0.9	0.8
Other official claims on countries denominated in the debtor's own currency	0.9	1.0	0.9	1.6	1.5	2.7	3.8	4.6
Official foreign exchange claims arising from swap credits and related assistance	0.7	—	—	0.4	1.6[c]	1.3[c]	1.5[c]	1.2[c]
Identified official holdings of Eurocurrencies								
Eurodollars								
Industrial countries	5.1	3.4	5.6	7.3	6.5	7.0	7.9	14.7
Primary producing countries								
More developed countries	1.6	1.7	3.2	3.4	3.0	3.8	3.7	4.8
Less developed countries	3.8	5.4	9.2	10.3	22.8	27.7	34.0	38.5
Western Hemisphere	1.0	1.6	3.6	4.0	5.0	5.6	5.9	7.3
Middle East	0.6	1.1	1.9	2.3	12.0	16.7	19.1	20.6
Asia	1.1	1.1	2.0	2.7	3.0	3.5	5.9	7.8
Africa	1.1	1.6	1.7	1.3	2.8	2.0	3.1	2.9
Memorandum item: Major oil-exporting countries	1.6	2.8	3.9	4.0	15.6	20.7	23.7	25.8
Total identified Eurodollars	10.5	10.4	18.0	21.1	32.3	38.5	45.6	58.0

Other Eurocurrencies	0.4	1.1	3.2	5.3	5.8	7.2	7.6	12.3
Total identified holdings of Eurocurrencies	10.9	11.6	21.2	26.4	38.0	45.7	53.1	70.3
Identified claims on World Bank (IBRD) and International Development Agency (IDA)	0.7	0.6	0.6	0.9	0.9	1.8	2.5	2.1
Residual[d]	1.0	6.2	6.3	7.7	10.4	7.1	12.1	9.3
Total official holdings of foreign exchange	45.4	75.1	96.1	102.0	126.9	137.5	160.6	201.2

[a] Includes the estimated change in the value of holdings owing to the general realignment of currencies in 1971, the U.S. dollar devaluation in 1973, and the widespread floating of currencies since 1974.

[b] Covers only claims of countries, including those denominated in the claimant's own currency.

[c] Comprises the double deposit arrangement between the Deutsche Bundesbank and the Bank of Italy.

[d] Part of this residual occurs because some member countries do not classify all the foreign exchange claims that they report to the fund. It also includes asymmetries arising because data on U.S. and U.K. currency liabilities are more comprehensive than data on official foreign exchange as shown in *International Financial Statistics*, from which data in this table are drawn.

SOURCE: International Monetary Fund, *Annual Report*, 1978, table 16, p. 53.

pluses in the 1930s. Thus a major focus of international discussions was on the need for countries to be willing to bear their "fair share" of the collective oil deficit.[65]

Although some countries, such as Japan, were widely viewed as behaving in an excessively mercantilist manner, for most countries the willingness to run trade and current account deficits was much greater than had been anticipated. With the acceleration of world inflation, avoiding the effects of exchange-rate declines in increasing prices had become an important political goal in many countries. As a consequence, many countries borrowed heavily to limit the depreciation of their currencies. While largely removing the danger of a mercantilist scramble for surpluses, the appetite of some countries running deficits soon became itself a source of concern.

International monetary officials recognized that initially it was much safer to err on the side of too much financing than of too much adjustment. As time went on, however, concern grew that some countries were putting off needed adjustments unduly. This concern, combined with the continued large growth in international reserve aggregates, gave rise to renewed worries about uncontrolled expansion of international liquidity. Indeed, although floating exchange rates had been adopted, because of the increased magnitude of underlying disequilibrium, official intervention in the foreign exchange markets was much greater in aggregate than for comparable lengths of time during the pegged rate system of the 1960s, and the proportion of "controlled" international liquidity continued to decline.[66]

It became fashionable to argue that international liquidity was now demand-determined and that, by analogy to domestic monetary theory and the real bills doctrine, this would be likely to result in an unstable inflationary process.[67] As I have argued elsewhere, however, this analogy is misleading.[68] Demand-determined international reserve accumulation through official borrowing and/or running a balance-of-payments surplus is quite a different matter from the operation of a domestic monetary policy on the basis of accommodating the growth in the demand for money at below-equilibrium interest rates. The latter causes a cumulative inflation spiral because economic

---

[65] For discussions on, and for references to the literature on, this episode and on the deficit sharing proposals, see Robert Solomon, "The Allocation of 'Oil Deficits,' " *Brookings Papers on Economic Activity*, no. 1 (Washington, D.C.: Brookings Institution, 1975), pp. 61–87; Willett, *The Oil Transfer Problem*; and Willett, *Floating Exchange Rates*, chap. 4.

[66] "Controlled" international liquidity refers to noncurrency reserve assets and to reserve positions in the IMF. See OECD, *Economic Outlook* (July 1978), p. 53.

[67] See, for example, Tom de Vries, "Jamaica, or the Non-Reform of the International Monetary System," *Foreign Affairs*, vol. 54, no. 3 (April 1976), pp. 577–605.

[68] Willett, *Floating Exchange Rates*.

66

actors are not given correct signals and monetary authorities respond to maintain a disequilibrium situation by expanding the money supply too rapidly.

The most appropriate international liquidity analogy to the real bills doctrine would be determining the allocation of SDRs on this criterion. In the current system, however, the demand-determined expansion of international liquidity places an opportunity cost on the acquisition of reserves. To acquire "uncontrolled" international liquidity, a country must pay the price either of forgoing current absorption by running a balance-of-payments surplus or of borrowing from the international financial markets on commercial terms. Thus, contrary to what is sometimes implied, such reserve accumulations do not by any means free countries entirely from external discipline. As will be discussed below, the amount of discipline generated through these decentralized mechanisms may not always be optimal from the standpoint of the most efficient operation of the international monetary system, but it should not be overlooked. It should also be remembered that demand-determined reserve creation is not something new. Indeed, it formed a major part of reserve creation throughout the Bretton Woods system. Furthermore, as our previous analysis argued, it was the uncontrolled supply portion of international liquidity expansion that created the really serious problems, not the uncontrolled demand creation.

What is largely new about demand-determined reserve creation is its huge magnitude and the fact that much of it in recent years has been created by borrowing from private markets rather than by running balance-of-payments surpluses. These factors make it quite understandable that many have become concerned that there is continuing to be excessive creation of international liquidity and that this may be a major factor contributing to world inflation. Closer analysis suggests, however, that it is not at all clear that the world economy would have operated better if there had been substantially less international liquidity creation since 1972.

An Ideal Solution to the Interrelationship between International Liquidity and Adjustment Policies

As has been emphasized a number of times, simple analogies between changes in international reserve totals and world economic performance can be highly misleading. The effects of international liquidity creation must be analyzed within the context of the overall operation of the international adjustment process. The effects of a given increase in aggregate reserves may vary greatly depending on both the causes of the increases and how they are distributed. Although many have expressed fears that excessive access to international liquidity generated excessive world inflation, much concern was also expressed that a number of countries, such as Germany, Japan, and Switzerland, were running too large a trade or current account surplus. Such conflicting complaints suggest that from the standpoint of the overall operation of the adjustment process, aggregate international liquidity was neither obviously too abundant nor obviously too scarce.

Concern that there needed to be a great deal of adjustment by both surplus and deficit countries is not a signal of aggregate reserve imbalances, but rather reflects either differing judgments about desirable balance-of-payments patterns or the need to improve the operation of the adjustment process. Except when there is a clear imbalance of pressures placed on surplus and deficit countries, variations in the rate of growth of aggregate international liquidity cannot be used to improve the operation of the adjustment process. This problem must be attacked directly through international surveillance of the adjustment process.

Considerations of how best to try to undertake such international surveillance lie beyond the scope of this study.[69] The point here is that *with effective international surveillance, concerns about excessive access to international liquidity become irrelevant.* Of course, as will be discussed below, international surveillance is not fully effective, and mechanisms for liquidity control can thus play a useful supplementary role. The important point is that such issues can be approached more productively from the standpoint of aiding the operation of the surveillance process than from the standpoint of gaining better control of international liquidity aggregates.

In a well-functioning international monetary system, international surveillance should be the primary method of keeping both surplus and deficit countries from unduly delaying needed adjustments. The problem of international liquidity would be to assure that financing was available for cases in which it was generally agreed that adjustment should be delayed or deficient behavior by private speculation should be supplemented or offset as the case might be.[70]

---

[69] For my own views on this topic, and for extensive references to the literature on this subject, see ibid., chap. 4, and Thomas D. Willett, "Alternative Approaches to International Surveillance of Exchange-Rate Policies," in *Managed Exchange-Rate Flexibility* (Proceedings of a conference sponsored by the Federal Reserve Bank of Boston, October 1978), pp. 148–72.

[70] In the case of destabilizing speculation, one would want to offset its effects, whereas if the problem were an insufficiency of stabilizing private speculation, one would want to supplement the operation of these forces. Of course, in practice, it may be very hard to identify clearly such speculative deficiencies. See, for example, Logue, Sweeney, and Willett, "The Speculative Behavior of Exchange Rates," and Willett, *Floating Exchange Rates*, chap. 2.

From this perspective, the primary focus of international liquidity management should be on providing financing where needed.

As long as a system of universal freely floating rates is rejected, such official international liquidity will be needed in two kinds of cases: (1) to help countries, largely the lower-income developing countries, that have little effective access to the private international financial markets; and (2) to provide supplementary or lender-of-last-resort finance where delaying adjustment or offsetting current market forces is judged to be internationally socially desirable, but private lenders are not willing to provide finance, at least at normal commercial rates. The first consideration would call for a regular growth of SDRs or some other official source of finance while the latter considerations would call for discretionary (and usually conditional) lending authority by the IMF. A reasonable, though controversial, case can also be made for relying primarily on SDR creation to provide the secular growth in demand for reserves by countries who enjoy regular access to private international financial markets. (This issue will be considered in part 3.)

The major point is that the ideal operation of the international monetary system would have international surveillance determine the desirable pattern of adjustment actions. The international liquidity problem would be to assure that adequate financing was available when official intervention by deficit countries was called for. From this perspective, if deficit countries were unduly avoiding undertaking needed adjustments by borrowing excessively from private financial markets, the appropriate response would be direct pressure from the IMF on these countries to adjust more and borrow less, not some attempt to reduce aggregate international liquidity. The latter is usually much too blunt an instrument to be an effective method of influencing the operation of the international adjustment process.

Of course, international surveillance of the adjustment process does not work perfectly by any means. The effective power of the International Monetary Fund to influence the adjustment policies of its member countries is limited, as is the influence of less inclusive organizations such as the OECD and the Group of Ten and ad hoc international and bilateral exercises in moral suasion and bargaining. Where international surveillance is not fully effective, access to borrowing from the private international financial markets can allow countries to run larger and/or longer deficits than the international community would judge desirable.

In this connection several points should be made, however. First, the best way to reduce the amount of deficiencies that result from this process is to try to improve the operation of international surveillance of the adjustment process, not to attempt to exert greater control over international liquidity aggregates. Countries are, of course, quite zealous about the amount of effective power to control their exchange rate and balance-of-payments adjustment actions that they are willing to give up to an international body. Part of the attraction of some schemes for more centralized control of aggregate international liquidity may be the hope that greater centralized control of the adjustment process may be slipped in by the back door than could be achieved directly. I am doubtful that this is a promising approach, however.

Second, as was discussed earlier, to the extent that excessive borrowing takes place, other countries under floating rates have relatively greater scope to protect themselves from the importation of serious inflationary pressures.

Third, the actual amount of international deficit financing that has occurred in recent years would probably not have been significantly lower if formal IMF approval of all official borrowing from the private international financial markets had been required. In almost all of the cases of such private borrowing on a significant scale, the countries in question were also receiving discretionary official loans from the IMF. In such cases, if the IMF had judged that the overall amount of a country's borrowing was too great, the IMF could have refused to grant official loans. Thus it is doubtful that, in practice, access to borrowing from private financial markets has seriously undercut the degree of international discipline placed on deficit countries as much as many have argued. Judgments that many countries were allowed to postpone adjustment for too long must largely imply a belief that the IMF and other sources of official loans were too lenient—that is, that the controller of the system erred, not that uncontrolled access to international credit allowed countries to escape the IMF discipline.

To some extent such judgments, with which I agree, are a reflection of beliefs that it was better to err on the side of underadjustment rather than overadjustment. As noted earlier, this was definitely the prudent side on which to err initially. A second aspect is that the IMF undoubtedly lent more funds than it would have ideally wished and was able to secure less in the way of commitments to adjustment actions than it would have preferred. This was because in countries like the United Kingdom and particularly Italy, governments faced severe political pressures to delay adjustments and feared that the policies the IMF would have preferred on economic grounds would result in political instability, or at a minimum significantly reduced chances of reelection. In such circumstances, the likely outcome of IMF surveillance is less adjustment than the IMF would like, but more than would be undertaken in the absence of IMF involvement.

Given such inevitable political limitations on IMF surveillance, each access to private financing does reduce IMF leverage and can contribute to balance-of-payments financing that is excessive from the standpoint of the efficient operation of the international monetary system. Probably the best solution, however, is careful monitoring of official borrowing from private markets and the initiation of warnings against excessive borrowings at an early stage. One suspects that the informal word that the IMF was growing concerned about the level of a country's official borrowing could increase the cost and reduce the availability of private international credit to such a country. Although I am more sanguine than many have been about the problems in this area, it is certainly important that the interrelationships between IMF surveillance and lending policies and official access to private international credit receive a great deal of attention.

A final consideration is whether official borrowing from private international financial markets should be allowed at all. A prohibition would provide at least some increase in centralized control and would contribute to a more tidy blueprint of the international monetary system. Indeed, on such grounds one can make a strong case for allowing only SDRs to be used as international reserves (over and above some level of working balances required for actual exchange market intervention).

There are several arguments against such an approach, however. It clearly interferes with the individual choice of nations and on basic liberal principles one would be hesitant to prescribe such restraints unless they are required to avoid severe adverse effects on other countries or on the system as a whole. The preceding analysis has suggested that the costs of allowing individual choice in this area has not been nearly as great as many have implied. Thus when approached from a liberal perspective rather than a central planning perspective, the case for learning to live with considerable official access to private financial markets looks much stronger.

This consideration is reinforced if one considers the problems of attempting to secure agreement on such prohibitions and of enforcing such agreements if they could be achieved. Agreements among sovereign nations to limit their freedom of action are difficult to achieve. The supply of international cooperative actions is far from unlimited. Thus it seems reasonable to attempt to save efforts at agreement on strong international prohibitions for areas in which the prospective aggregate benefits generated are the greatest. Based on the preceding analysis, it is doubtful that the prospective aggregate benefits from the greater control of international liquidity that might result would be sufficient to put such prohibitions high on the agenda of needs for international action. In terms of politically adverse effects from decentralized decision making, the problem of potential instability due to reserve switching that will be discussed in chapter 3 would seem to be of much greater importance.

Two additional points might be noted here. One is that the private markets' judgments about willingness to lend can give useful information to officials responsible for international liquidity and adjustment surveillance. The other is that such access has greatly reduced a major aspect of the asymmetrical position of reserve currency countries—the extent of their differential borrowing privileges. Today many countries have the ability to run balance-of-payments deficits without running down their reserves or borrowing from the IMF. Most of these countries do still have to pay somewhat higher interest rates on such borrowing than does the United States, but the difference in positions for many countries is substantially less than a decade ago. It should also be remembered that the members of this new class of borrowers are able to borrow largely at their own discretion, while the borrowing resulting from the key currency portion of the dollar comes largely at the discretion of other countries, thus offsetting at least somewhat the U.S. advantages of borrowing at lower rates.

Developments in 1976–1978: A Final Example of the Need to Look beyond the Behavior of Reserve Aggregates

International reserve aggregates have continued to grow rapidly since the oil shock. The causes of and distribution of reserve increases have changed substantially, however. The rate of accumulation by the OPEC countries has slowed considerably, as has the amount of borrowing by deficit countries to limit the decline of the levels of their international reserve holdings. At the same time, however, the U.S. balance-of-payments position began to worsen again as oil import payments continued to increase and the nonoil trade balance deteriorated in response to more rapid economic recovery in the United States than abroad and the acceleration of inflationary pressures in the United States. The resulting pressures on the foreign exchange market led to substantial official intervention to moderate the magnitude of exchange-rate changes.[71] The United Kingdom used the

---

[71] For further discussion on the worsened position of the dollar over this period, see Thomas D. Willett, "The Fall and Rise of the Dollar" (Testimony before the Subcommittee on International Economics of the Joint Economic Committee, U.S. Congress, December 14, 1978), also available as AEI Reprint No. 96 (Washington, D.C.: American Enterprise Institute, 1979); and Thomas D. Willett, "It's Too Easy To Blame the Speculators," *Euromoney* (May 1979), pp. 111–20.

market strength of the pound to replenish its seriously depleted net international liquidity position, adding almost SDR 14 billion to its reserves during 1977. Both this and the more than SDR 3 billion increase in reserves for Italy were clearly desirable developments from the standpoint of achieving better balance in the world economy.

The substantial reserve increases by Germany and Japan were of considerably more questionable desirability, however. From the perspective of many U.S. financial officials, these increases during 1976 and 1977 were undesirable attempts by these surplus countries to maintain their surplus positions. This was leading to a serious overvaluation of the dollar and an excessive concentration of the counterpart of the OPEC surplus on countries that were not in the financial position to accumulate substantially larger debts. From this perspective, these reserve accumulations represented a threat to international financial stability.

As is indicated in table 7, aggregate reserve growth sped up during 1976 and 1977, increasing by SDR 28 billion and SDR 40 billion respectively, as contrasted with a growth of a little over SDR 14 billion in 1975. In 1978, aggregate reserve increases dropped sharply, to approximately SDR 15 billion, but the reserve increases of the financially strongest industrial countries accelerated. While the aggregate reserves of the OPEC countries actually dropped, the reserves of Germany, Japan, and Switzerland soared, increasing by SDR 8.7 billion, SDR 6.5 billion, and SDR 5.2 billion, respectively. Thus, although the aggregate rate of reserve increases during 1978 looked more reasonable by historical standards, from the previous perspective the international financial balance worsened rather than improved during 1978.

German and Japanese officials had quite a different perspective, however. They maintained that they were not intervening to maintain undervalued currencies, but only to promote stable market conditions. They were leaning against the wind to offset perceived tendencies of the private market to generate exaggerated exchange-rate swings. Thus, although their exchange market intervention and reserve accumulation did reflect international financial imbalances, these actions were seen as contributing to international financial stability and avoiding disorderly market conditions, rather than as being the cause of imbalance.

My own judgment concerning these events falls between these contrasting positions. The case that the exchange-rate pressures resulted largely from disequilibrating private speculation is not nearly as strong as the surplus countries (especially Japan) argued. There was certainly a strong tendency in Japan to define exchange market

TABLE 7

INTERNATIONAL RESERVE TOTALS, 1973–1978
(end of period, millions of SDRs)

Country	1973	1974	1975	1976	1977	1978
All countries	152,069	179,522	193,780	221,548	261,668	277,007
Industrial countries	95,748	97,935	104,112	113,483	139,420	160,392
United States	11,919	13,115	13,567	15,768	15,965	15,032
Canada	4,782	4,758	4,549	5,029	3,793	3,507
Japan	10,151	11,042	10,947	19,149	19,149	25,714
Austria	2,382	2,801	3,796	3,494	3,494	4,611
Belgium	4,228	4,366	4,952	4,743	4,743	4,535
Denmark	1,098	764	749	788	1,375	2,471
France	7,070	7,230	10,757	8,392	8,392	10,692
Germany	27,497	26,461	26,510	29,954	32,713	41,360
Italy	5,335	5,669	4,078	5,727	9,573	11,380
Netherlands	5,426	5,682	6,073	6,358	6,639	5,822
Norway	1,306	1,575	1,911	1,919	1,811	2,209
Sweden	2,096	1,418	2,628	2,144	3,020	3,376
Switzerland	7,063	7,360	8,908	11,385	11,385	16,550
United Kingdom	5,368	5,667	4,663	17,335	17,355	13,100
Oil-exporting countries	12,033	38,384	48,292	56,149	62,152	45,915
Other less developed countries	24,389	25,884	26,047	36,146	44,188	50,725

SOURCE: *International Financial Statistics* (Washington, D.C.: International Monetary Fund, various issues).

stability in terms of the constancy of nominal exchange rates, rather than whether rates were moving toward or away from equilibrium, and there was a great deal of support for the belief that it was important to maintain an export surplus. Germany displayed similar tendencies, although to a much less degree. I suspect that the views of U.S. officials on equilibrium exchange rates were more nearly correct, but many U.S. officials probably also overestimated the damage to the stability of the system threatened by the continued German and Japanese current account surpluses and failed to distinguish sufficiently between balance-of-payments positions resulting from market forces and from government policies.[72] Likewise some U.S. statements tended to give a considerably exaggerated view of the benefits to international monetary stability being generated by the shift of the

---

[72] For further discussion on this point, see Thomas D. Willett, "It's Too Simple to Blame the Countries with a Surplus," *Euromoney* (February 1978), pp. 89–96.

U.S. trade position into substantial deficit. Not long after, the worsening of the U.S. balance-of-payments position became generally acknowledged to be adversely rather than favorably affecting international financial stability.

The major point for this study, however, is not to attempt to determine who was right, but rather to illustrate that these reserve accumulations needed to be judged in terms of views of the operation of the international adjustment process, not in terms of norms for rates of reserve growth. This requires detailed knowledge about the distribution and causes of such changes. As has been indicated in the last several sections, although the rate of international reserve increases has been unusually high by historical standards in almost every year since 1970, when Bretton Woods entered the last stages of its breakdown, the causes and distribution of these increases have changed significantly over this period. In judging the effects and desirability of such changes, one must carefully evaluate their relationship to the operation of the international adjustment process on a disaggregate basis.

The international adjustment process has far too many important short-term consequences to leave the international control of its operation to the long-run regulator of the rate of international reserve increases, even if the long-run effectiveness of this approach were not open to the serious questions raised in earlier sections. On the other hand, when the problem of international supervision of the adjustment process is confronted directly, then the basis for concerns about the behavior of reserve aggregates largely disappears.

This conclusion does not imply that there are no important international liquidity issues, however. In the following chapter a number of current international liquidity issues will be addressed from the perspective developed in the preceding analysis.

3

Some Current Major
International Liquidity Issues

The Never-Ending Search for International Monetary Reform

There can hardly be an area for which there has been more conflicting advice offered, and more proposals penned, than that of international monetary reform. Many different types of interests are affected, and there are many different concepts of the objectives of the international monetary system. As a result, one can safely forecast that although events may cause the strength of cries for international monetary reform to rise and fall, substantive disagreement over the adequacy, much less the optimality, of existing international monetary arrangements will never be entirely eliminated.

Some of the disagreements surround issues of technical economic analysis. Views on how well floating rates have worked differ substantially depending on whether one views the observed volatility of exchange rates as resulting primarily from the instability of underlying economic fundamentals or from perceived inherent tendencies of private market speculation to magnify all out of proportion the effects of disturbances and generate chaotic conditions in their own right. Over time, there is some scope for accumulating evidence to narrow the range of substantive differences of view. It is obvious now, for example, that the adoption of floating rates need not generate a resurgence of the economic warfare and crippling of world trade of the 1930s that some critics of floating had prophesized. Thus we might say that floating rates have proved themselves to be a *feasible* basis for a functioning monetary order.

Conflicts of views on the *desirability* of floating rates and on the degree of desirable official management of exchange rates have not narrowed nearly so much, however. Recent history has not given us the basis for a simple and unambiguous interpretation of how well floating rates have worked. The simple facts do not accord with only a single interpretation, obvious to all reasonable observers, as would have been the case if floating rates were accompanied by a high degree of stability in underlying world economic conditions. As a consequence, distinguishing between cause and effect becomes no easy matter. Various types of technical economic analysis can narrow the range of uncertainty about interpretations, but even the results of the most advanced economic analysis at present leaves some range of ambiguity. Furthermore, such analysis often does not appear to influence the major disputants.

In part this may be because the analysis is often complicated, but more often I fear it is due to the natural human tendency to render our interpretations of the facts consistent with our perceived notions. With some exceptions, there has really been remarkably little switching of views between those who were initially favorably predisposed toward floating and those who were largely critical. It is important, though, that few of those critical of floating would now advocate a return to a full-fledged adjustable peg system like Bretton Woods. I take as an article of faith that while experience and technical analysis do not quickly change strongly held views, they do gradually influence views and help to narrow the range of controversies among responsible individuals and policy makers.

Control over International Liquidity

The Misplaced Focus on Controlling International Liquidity Aggregates. As with the debate over the exchange-rate system, one cannot expect debate over the control of international liquidity to cease soon, nor should it. It is my hope, however, that the terms of debate in this area will gravitate toward a more satisfactory framework of analysis than has underlain many of the charges that the generation of international liquidity under our new international monetary system is almost completely out of control and that this in turn has been a major cause of world inflation in recent years.

As has been argued in some detail in the preceding chapter, the most reasonable charge, that deficient international monetary arrangements have been a major cause of world inflation, applied to the last years of the old pegged exchange-rate system, not to our new system based on more flexible exchange rates. Even in that case, statements about the magnitude of the inflationary effects of the failures of the operation of the international monetary system have often been greatly exaggerated. Although the huge expansion of the Eurocurrency markets and official international reserves has been temporarily associated with a substantial acceleration of the rate of world inflation, more comprehensive analysis suggests that this acceleration has been due less to the cause-and-effect scenarios posited by some of the simple (perhaps I should say naive) versions of international reserve monetarism than many have argued.

Nothing in this analysis suggests that proper management of national monetary aggregates is not important for securing economic stability. Thus the results of this study are not in any broad sense antimonetarist, but they do strongly suggest that a simply global focus on control of international reserve and Eurocurrency aggregates is not a sound basis for restoring global economic stability. The distribution of international liquidity and the causes of its creation are as important as the value of its global aggregate. For example, the creation of international liquidity through the undesired payments imbalances associated with the breakdown of the Bretton Woods system placed much greater direct inflationary pressure on recipient countries—that is, they were more difficult to sterilize—than do SDR allocations and increases in the market price of gold. Similarly, the second-round effects of such international liquidity creation will vary greatly depending on whether the increases accrue primarily to reserve sinks like Germany or Saudi Arabia, or to countries that are constrained by balance-of-payments problems and would quickly spend their increased reserves. Appropriate levels and distribution of international liquidity can only be determined on the basis of a careful disaggregate analysis of the operation of the adjustment process. For example, if after the oil shock the expansion of international liquidity were limited to a normal trend rate of growth, the consequent worldwide recession probably would have been much more severe, and the resort to trade restrictions and competitive exchange-rate manipulation would have been much more widespread. The best approach to improving the operation of the international monetary system is through direct surveillance of the international adjustment process, and not restoration of convertibility or asset settlement.

Indeed, most international liquidity issues can only be analyzed properly in relation to the operation of the international adjustment process. Thus many of the concerns about lack of control of international liquidity are relevant only to the extent that direct multilateral surveillance of the adjustment process through the IMF and other forums is not working well. With a well-functioning process for international surveillance and management of the adjustment process, the main function of international liquidity management would be to assure that international liquidity was available for the support of exchange rates and the financing of balance-of-payments deficits that were deemed internationally desirable or at least acceptable.

Of course, international surveillance of the adjustment process does not work ideally, so international liquidity considerations can influence the operation of the adjustment process where differences of view about policies are present. A country with ample owned reserves or access to borrowing from the private market has more power to run a larger and more prolonged balance-of-payments deficit against the judgment of international officials than does a country that is more dependent on discretionary financing from the IMF. Thus in the actual operation of the international monetary system, international liquidity considerations are not irrelevant to the operation of exchange-rate policies and the adjustment process. However, when dealing with such issues as gaining better international control of official borrowing from private markets, proposals labeled as attempting to gain better control over international liquidity would be identical for the most part to the ways in which one might hope to strengthen international surveillance of the adjustment process. Viewed from either perspective, the objective would be to strengthen the ability of the IMF to discourage "excessive" official borrowing from the private international capital markets. In my judgment efforts to deal with such problems are likely to be more effective if they focus more directly on the supervision of the operation of the adjustment process than on control of international liquidity aggregates.

The restoration of convertibility into reserve assets and particularly mandatory asset settlement, as proposed in the early stages of the post-floating international monetary reform negotiations, would facilitate the control over international reserve aggregates, but the resulting effects on adjustment pressures would probably be haphazard. To improve global economic performance, it is much more sensible to focus international attention directly on the operation of the adjustment process and allow flexibility in the resulting international reserve aggregates than to focus primarily on the behavior of reserve aggregates and leave the operation of the adjustment process and distribution of reserves to work themselves out as they may. There is not the degree of automaticity in the balance-of-payments adjustment behavior for changes in reserve aggregates to represent an efficient mechanism for controlling the operation of the international adjustment mechanism.

In the process of international surveillance, it will be desirable to focus attention on the behavior of a wide range of net and gross reserve indicators for each country, but a simple pure reserve indicator role such as was proposed by the United States in the negotiations of the Committee of Twenty would be unlikely to prove adequate (or politically acceptable). Detailed discussion of how best to approach international surveillance of the adjustment process goes beyond the scope of this study. Moreover, achieving stronger international surveillance will be no easy matter. But this is the direction from which to approach the issue of gaining better control over the international aspects of the operation of the world economy.[1]

Official Borrowing from Private Markets. Official access to borrowing from private financial markets does not allow nearly as much escape from balance-of-payments discipline as many have feared. The private market does impose a discipline of its own, as evidenced by the higher interest rates and the reduced access to credit that face countries judged to be poorer financial risks. Of course, the standards for lending by commercial bankers are unlikely to coincide precisely with those for the most desirable operation of the international adjustment process. We cannot reasonably rely on commercial lending policies alone to provide and manage international liquidity. A clear example is the provision of balance-of-payments financing for the numerical majority of developing countries whose financial situations do not give them effective access to commercial markets. Likewise, as noted above, it is possible for nations to escape official international discipline through commercial borrowing. The magnitude of problems of this latter kind has often been greatly exaggerated, however. There is likely to be a strong interdependence between commercial and official lending policies; commercial institutions are extremely hesitant to lend to borrowers whose access to official credit has been terminated. In almost all cases of large balance-of-payments financing from the private markets, the borrowing country has also had access at the same time to official lending or standby arrangements.

Clearly there have been situations in which countries have prolonged adjustment for too long as judged ex post, but seldom has this occurred as a result of official borrowing from the private market in opposition to pressure from the IMF. Thus most past cases of excessive financing can be ascribed at least as much to inappropriate national and international management as to a lack of official control

---

[1] I have discussed approaches to international surveillance of the adjustment process in Thomas D. Willett, *Floating Exchange Rates and International Monetary Reform* (Washington, D.C.: American Enterprise Institute, 1977), chap. 4, and in Thomas D. Willett, "Alternative Approaches to International Surveillance of Exchange-Rate Policies," in *Managed Exchange-Rate Flexibility: Proceedings of a Conference Sponsored by the Federal Reserve Bank of Boston* (October 1978), pp. 148–72. These works contain extensive references to the literature on this subject.

over international liquidity. As noted in the previous chapter, however, given the limits on IMF political leverage, the interrelationships between IMF and private lending policies can be of considerable importance and should receive a good deal of attention.

It should also be remembered that appropriate balance-of-payments financing is not an unambiguous concept. In my judgment, charges of excessive uncontrolled international liquidity have usually had more to do with disagreements about what are appropriate policies than about genuine and serious deficiencies in current institutional arrangements.

International Monetary Stability and the Tightness of International Monetary Organization

A major thesis of this study is that various bureaucratic, political, and economic incentives make the current international monetary arrangements a great deal more stable than many critics have argued. The principal source of policy inconsistencies in the postwar international monetary system has been the tendency to delay adjustment with sticky exchange rates, not the problem of overadjustments that occurred in the 1930s. The adoption of more flexible exchange rates has substantially reduced this problem. Of course, we do not have a system of completely freely floating exchange rates. Even if we did, it would not automatically eliminate all possibilities of policy conflicts and inconsistent balance-of-payments and exchange-rate policies that can threaten international monetary stability. Nor do we have the kind of centralized control or clearcut standards for acceptable behavior and effective sanctions against deviations that assure policy consistency and system stability.

Still, however, the combination of the adoption of substantial exchange-rate flexibility, the development of a basic fabric of international cooperation and the perceived interests of the major countries in avoiding extreme monetary instability, and the maintenance of a relatively passive balance-of-payments policy by the United States have been sufficient so far to prevent the problems of policy inconsistencies from reaching severe dimensions. Although some might view the current loosely structured system as a *free-for-all* regime that is likely to repeat the severe instabilities of the 1930s, this system is in fact a reasonably workable compromise between a number of extreme prototypes for international monetary organization.[2]

---

[2] For recent discussions of various basic organizing principles for the international monetary system, see Benjamin J. Cohen, *Organizing the World's Money: The Political Economy of International Monetary Relations* (New York: Basic Books, 1977); Richard N. Cooper, "Prolegomena to the Choice of an International Monetary System," in C. Fred

Desires for Tight International Control. It is easy to construct pure international monetary systems that would be logically consistent. The major problem is that all such systems require countries to cede substantial amounts of traditional national sovereignty to automatic rules or discretionary international authority, or to the maintenance of perceived hegemony by the United States. There have been two major types of motivation behind proposals for tightly structured international monetary systems. One is the desire for logical purity to assure that the institutional framework contains certain solutions for all possible problems. The second motivation stems from beliefs that a relatively decentralized system will provide the United States with unfair economic, political, and prestige benefits from the operation of the international monetary system.

Although many critics exaggerate the special benefits to the United States from an international monetary system that is not highly centralized, they do correctly perceive that under such a system the dollar does tend in Orwellian terms to be "more equal" than other currencies. Because of the payment of competitive rates of interest on most foreign dollar holdings, it is doubtful that the United States receives any substantial disproportionate net economic benefits from such a system, but to the many concerned primarily with political and prestige factors, this is of little consequence.

Bergsten and L. B. Krause, eds., *World Politics and International Economics* (Washington, D.C.: Brookings Institution, 1975); and Fred Hirsch, Michael Doyle, and Edward L. Morse, *Alternatives to Monetary Disorder* (New York: McGraw-Hill, 1977). Cohen, for example, lists the following as basic organizing principles for international monetary management, in addition to a free-for-all regime without any organizing rules: automaticity (a gold standard, for example, or freely floating rates); supranationality (with the IMF as a true international central bank); hegemony (a pure dollar standard and one that many would argue characterized the early postwar operation of the Bretton Woods system); and negotiation. Of course, as these authors recognize, actual systems tend to be based on combinations of the basic organizing principles. Thus, for example, although I believe that the United States should display a large element of benign neglect toward our balance of payments and exchange, I do not think it is feasible to rely entirely on a passive U.S. policy to solve the so-called nth country or consistency problem among national balance-of-payments and exchange-rate policies. As indicated in Willett, *Floating Exchange Rates,* and in Willett, "International Surveillance of Exchange-Rate Policies," my own judgment on this score is that the best practical solution to this problem is a combination of judgmental international guidelines with a great deal of passivity on the part of the United States. As indicated by some of the reviews of my recent book, there is far from complete agreement on this score. Ronald I. McKinnon, in "Review of Floating Exchange Rates and International Monetary Reform," *Journal of Economic Literature,* vol. 16, no. 4 (December 1978), pp. 1469–73, for example, continued to argue for a pure passive policy that would make international guidelines unnecessary, whereas Giorgio Basevi, in "Review of Floating Exchange Rates and International Monetary Reform," *Journal of International Economics,* vol. 9, no. 1 (February 1979), pp. 143–46, found fault with my analysis on the opposite grounds that greater emphasis was needed on international rules.

The Political Infeasibility of a Tight System of International Control.
In trying to construct a highly structured system based on the restoration of exchange-rate pegging and convertibility of all currencies into reserve assets, the Committee of Twenty was motivated both by concerns to cut the role of the dollar down to size and to provide a logically consistent solution to all potential major international monetary problems. As John Williamson has convincingly argued, the decision to include a return to a par value system as a part of the committee's reform package doomed the original exercise to failure.[3] Even within the context of managed flexibility, the negotiating history makes it clear that almost no country was willing to give up as much sovereignty over international monetary behavior as was needed to secure agreement on a tightly organized international monetary system.

The current system is more one dominated by multinational negotiation about the implementation of generally agreed-upon principles than it is a pure dollar hegemony as some politically concerned critics charge. It still provides the United States much greater freedom than many in other nations would prefer. Concern about the asymmetrical position of the dollar remains prevalent. The basic problem, however, is that to construct a meaningfully consistent and symmetrical system that placed substantially greater formal international discipline on the United States would require that many of the traditional areas of national prerogative of other countries would also have to be substantially more constrained. As the U.S. negotiators correctly argued, one could not expect to construct a durable system based on a restoration of convertibility into reserve assets without establishing much stronger central control over the operation of the adjustment process and the management of the composition of international reserves.

For most countries, unwillingness to accept the latter outweighed dislike of the former. This explains both why a highly centralized system was not adopted, and why criticism of major aspects of the current system are bound to be continued. Of course, people and governments always want to have their cake and eat it too, and recognition that this is impossible hardly stops them from lamenting about what is not obtained.

On strictly economic grounds, a strong case can be made for a highly centralized international monetary system. This would have strong international control over the operation of the adjustment proc-

---

[3] John Williamson, *The Failure of World Monetary Reform, 1971–74* (New York: New York University Press, 1977), p. 135.

ess and international financial arrangements based on the SDR or some new international fiat asset. The International Monetary Fund would take on more of the traditional functions and powers of a true central bank. Provided that such a system were operated sensibly, it could indeed be the best international monetary system on aggregate efficiency grounds.

It seems clear, however, that rightly or wrongly, national governments are unwilling to cede substantially greater amounts of explicit formal power either to international rules or to discretionary authority. In this regard, national governments appear to be extremely adverse to risks. Officials of almost any country can easily conceive of situations in which the creation of greater formal international control would hamper the conduct of desired national policies. I suspect that in the absence of serious imminent threats, this risk aversion creates a substantial bias against agreements to cede strong formal and detailed authority over various aspects of international monetary behavior. This is true even though countries are in fact willing to give weight to international moral suasion and to substantially reduce their propensities to engage in exploitive or destabilizing actions in response to such moral suasion.

The Workability of a Loose System. When one broadens the analysis to political economy rather than exclusively economic efficiency considerations, the presumption must be that political desires for at least nominal autonomy should be given weight as legitimate considerations. If nations prefer a great deal of continued national sovereignty, it is unrealistic to expect a highly centralized international monetary system to be acceptable.

Deviations from aggregate economic optimality are not sufficient to establish a need for international monetary reform. On the other hand, one does not need to be a naive economic idealist to recognize that there are dangers in assuming that whatever is currently politically feasible or expedient is therefore unambiguously desirable in a broader political economy context. Maximizing short-run political expediency is likely to result in short-sightedness and the substantial underprovision of collective goods such as international monetary stability.[4]

---

[4] For discussions of international monetary stability as a public good, see Cooper, "Choice of an International Monetary System"; Lawrence H. Officer and Thomas D. Willett, "Reserve-Asset Preferences and the Confidence Problem in the Crisis Zone," *Quarterly Journal of Economics*, vol. 83, no. 4 (November 1969), pp. 688–95; and Lawrence H. Officer and Thomas D. Willett, "The Interaction of Adjustment and Gold Conversion Policies in a Reserve-Currency System," *Western Economic Journal* (March 1970), pp. 47–60.

Responsible political economy analysis should deal not just with current expedience but also with longer-run considerations and the seriousness of potential inadequacies of current arrangements. On this score, there is little practical value in pointing out that current arrangements are not perfect according to some particular criteria, but there is considerable relevance to the longer-term analysis of directions for future policy evolution as current political constraints become more malleable over time. Likewise there is a need for analysis of potentially major shortcomings of current arrangements that, if uncorrected, may cause major problems in the future. There is also scope for offering proposals that may make modest improvements at relatively low cost and for both policy advocacy and for more dispassionate attempts at evaluating aspects of proposals on technical grounds.

There is, thus, no single correct set of guidelines for good political economy analysis. What is important is that the various types of analysis be carefully distinguished.[5] In this regard, the analysis in chapter 2 suggests that current arrangements for international liquidity are not nearly as deficient as many have argued. In other words, improvements may certainly be possible, but the new international monetary system accepted at Jamaica is in my judgment quite a reasonable one. It is by no means definitively complete, but it is not as seriously incomplete or defective as many advocates of highly centralized systems have argued.

Effects of International Capital Mobility in General

The analysis in this study also provides a framework for evaluating proposals for more marginal improvements in the operation of the international monetary system. A major difficulty with many proposals for specific reforms is that they attempt to solve a problem without considering the effects of the proposal and whether it would really do much to reduce the basic problems. In this vein, as discussed in chapter 2, many recommendations to control aspects of the operation of the Eurocurrency markets are based on incorrect or exaggerated views of the effects of the expansion of these markets. They also fail to recognize that controlling the Eurocurrency markets would do little to reduce international capital mobility, which is in fact often the major cause of concern. (Although most policy discussions inev-

[5] Williamson, *Failure of World Monetary Reform*, pp. 202–3, provides a good example of realistically indicating the importance of recommended reforms. While advocating a number of additions to the Jamaica Agreements, he concludes that it would be a pity, but not a disaster, if his recommendations were not adopted.

itably focus on the problems caused by international capital mobility, it is important to remember that such capital mobility provides substantial benefits as well.)

Similarly, attempts to reestablish convertibility into reserve assets and control of international reserve aggregates are often taken as proximate objectives without sufficient attention being paid to the actual full effects on the operation of the international monetary system. As was argued in chapter 2, control over reserve aggregates alone is not sufficient to establish efficient management of the international financial aspects of the world economy.

Neither would the establishment of required ratios of SDRs to countries' total reserve assets be an effective basis for establishing centralized control over global reserve aggregates.[6] The problem is that countries could not reasonably be expected to be responsible for offshore Eurocurrency transactions denominated in their currency. As was discussed in chapter 2, Eurocurrency transactions have to a considerable extent replaced U.S. balance-of-payments deficits as a source of "uncontrolled" international liquidity creation. To avoid unreasonable obligations on reserve currency countries, a workable system of mandatory convertibility into reserve assets would require strong international regulation of official lending and borrowing in the Eurocurrency and other offshore markets. This is an area in which halfway measures are most unlikely to be workable and may be positively harmful.[7]

The point is not that it is not technically feasible to design a tight

[6] Study of such an approach was recommended by H. Johannes Witteveen, "On the Control of International Liquidity," *IMF Survey*, vol. 4 (October 28, 1975), pp. 313–16, while he was managing director of the International Monetary Fund, but evaluations of the proposal were largely negative. See, for instance, Andrew D. Crockett, "Control over International Reserves," *IMF Staff Papers*, vol. 25, no. 1 (Washington, D.C.: International Monetary Fund, 1978), pp. 1–24; Peter B. Kenen, "Techniques to Control International Reserves," in Robert Mundell and Jacques J. Polak, eds., *The New International Monetary System* (New York: Columbia University Press, 1977), pp. 202–22; Robert Solomon, "Techniques to Control International Reserves," in ibid., pp. 185–201; Marina Whitman, "Techniques to Control International Reserves: Comment," in ibid., pp. 223–28; and John Williamson, "Techniques to Control International Reserves: Comment," in ibid., pp. 228–30. It appears to have been dropped from current consideration by the IMF. See the report on the March 1979 meeting of the Interim Committee of the Board of Governors of the IMF in the *IMF Survey* (March 19, 1979).

[7] In this respect, there is a strong analogy to national capital controls programs. Clearly, in the U.S. experience during the 1960s, a piecemeal approach did not work. In the initial limited applications of control and tax measures, each control on a particular type of capital flow was successful in reducing that category, but the effect was to deflect capital flows to other channels, rather than to reduce flows substantially. Only when the program was expanded to a substantial number of categories did it begin to have a major impact on aggregate net capital flows. See Gottfried Haberler and Thomas D. Willett, *U.S. Balance of Payments Policies and International Monetary Reform* (Washington, D.C.: American Enterprise Institute, 1968).

system of international control over international liquidity that would be economically workable as long as countries abided by the regulations. Rather the point is that for a tight convertibility-based system to be workable over the long run, a very high degree of centralized regulation and ceding of traditional national prerogatives to international control would be required. Although most of the major industrial countries were willing to agree in 1971 to limit new placements of reserves in the Eurocurrency markets as a method of reducing this source of uncontrolled international liquidity creation, most of the developing countries have adamantly rejected proposals to limit even partly their freedom to determine where and in what form to hold their international reserves.

There would seem to be little political support abroad for the degree of centralized control which would be required to make a new convertibility system workable. Nor would the United States be likely to favor such a system. Indeed, during the Committee of Twenty negotiations the United States steadfastly opposed proposals for mandatory asset settlement in favor of a looser system of general convertibility on demand. This system would have limitations on the convertibility rights of "excessive" accumulations by individual countries as defined by a reserve indicator system.

The stated reason for opposition to mandatory asset settlement was the need to provide elasticity in the system, although it was just this type of elasticity that the Europeans were trying to avoid. Conceptually, whatever elasticity was needed for financing unusual payments developments could be provided through discretionary lending facilities in the IMF. The real cause of U.S. opposition to mandatory asset settlement was that under this system the decisions on providing elasticity in particular cases would be made by the IMF. This would have required the United States to give up power to an international authority, which U.S. officials were no more prepared to do than the Europeans were willing to subject themselves to the formal rules for balance-of-payments adjustment proposed by the United States.

The Role of the SDR

A similar situation holds with respect to the generally agreed-upon objective of making the SDR the principal reserve asset of the international monetary system. The motivations behind this objective are basically the same as those discussed above for a highly centralized system in general. In a highly structured system with tight international controls, the SDR would be the obvious choice for the major reserve asset, and holdings of other reserves beyond working balances would best be phased out.

A good case can be made for making the SDR an asset that could also be held by private parties. This would allow official exchange-rate intervention directly in SDRs. But such a vision of the international monetary system will come to pass, if ever, only in the distant future.[8] In the next decade or two, SDR management can do little to establish better control over international liquidity.

This still does leave, however, the more explicitly political or prestige argument for using the SDR to cut down on the perceived hegemony and special privileges of the dollar. The creation of the SDR has probably served a useful purpose in increasing the perceived symbolic acceptability and political legitimacy of the current international monetary system. In this regard, we may expect continued lip service to strengthening the role of the SDR as the center of the system, but little action of major import.

Although the SDR is unlikely to play a substantially stronger role in the international monetary system over the next several decades, a strong case can be made for the recent decisions to begin again to create new SDRs. Perhaps the major argument against SDR creation is the belief that the world is already awash with too much international liquidity and that such SDR creation will only further fuel the flames of world inflation. Such views, however, usually rest on the type of international reserve monetarist views that were criticized in chapter 2.[9] The analysis in this study suggests that we do not at present have a substantial excess of aggregate international liquidity. It seems unlikely to me that moderate rates of SDR expansion would force any substantial amount of imported inflation on countries.

Continued moderate rates of SDR creation would have several advantages beyond the politically symbolic one of reducing the perceived special advantages and hegemony of the dollar and providing a less asymmetrical-appearing international monetary system. SDR creation would reduce the degree to which reserve centers would need to run balance-of-payments deficits to provide increases in the reserves of nonreserve currency countries.

---

[8] For analysis of SDR-based international monetary systems, see Fred Hirsch, *An SDR Standard: Impetus, Elements, and Impediments*, Princeton Essays in International Finance, no. 99 (Princeton, N.J.: International Finance Section, Princeton University, 1973); Cohen, *Organizing the World's Money*, chap. 6; and K. Alec Chrystal, *International Money and the Future of the SDR*, Princeton Essays in International Finance, no. 128 (Princeton, N.J.: International Finance Section, Princeton University, 1978).

[9] See also, however, the broader critique of further SDR creation offered by J. Carter Murphy in "SDRs, Dollars, and Other International Reserves" (Paper presented at the meeting of the Southwest Social Science Association, Fort Worth, Texas, March 30, 1979), and in *The International Monetary System* (Washington, D.C.: American Enterprise Institute, 1979).

It has become clear that, even with managed floating, most countries desire to see some rate of increase in their average levels of gross reserve holdings over time.[10] Given recent concern both at home and abroad about the U.S. balance-of-payments deficits, it would seem generally beneficial that the dollar not be subjected to a secular overvaluation on private accounts because of official demands for dollar accumulations. The other major reserve currency countries have made it clear that they do not seek substantially increased reserve currency roles. Thus there is a strong case for allowing SDR expansions to be the main method of secular increases in the demand for owned reserves, rather than forcing such demands to be met by increased holdings of reserve currencies.

To enhance the acceptability of the SDR there may be a case for further increasing the rate of return on SDRs. Although the original 1.5 percent rate of interest on SDRs was much too low, it is not clear that substantial further increases in SDR interest rates would be of major importance. The analysis in chapter 2 suggests that over a fairly wide range the rate of return on international reserves is not likely to have large effects on the behavior of the central banks of the major countries. With respect to the behavior of many of the smaller countries, however, this could be of significance. I also do not see a major need for changing the current method of valuing the SDR in terms of a weighted average of a basket of currencies.[11]

---

[10] As argued in chapter 2, the adoption of managed floating should cause a one-time reduction in the level of reserves demanded. It would not mean, however, that reserve demands would not continue to grow from this new, lower base. The initial generation of excess reserves would eliminate the need for reserve growth until these excess supplies were gone, but after that secular growth in reserves would again be desirable.

[11] See also, however, the recent critical analysis of this valuation procedure by Chrystal, *International Money and the Future of the SDR*, pp. 20–22. For further discussion of the interest rate and of the valuation of SDRs, see Jacob Dreyer, *Composite Reserve Assets in the International Monetary System* (Greenwich, Conn.: JAI Press, 1977); Jacques J. Polak, *Valuation and Rate of Interest of the SDR* (Washington, D.C.: International Monetary Fund, 1974); Edward Tower and Thomas D. Willett, "More on Official versus Market Financing of Payments Deficits and the Optimal Pricing of International Reserves," *Kyklos*, fasc. 3 (1972), pp. 537–52; John Williamson, "International Liquidity: A Survey," *Economic Journal*, vol. 83, no. 331 (September 1973), pp. 685–764; and Williamson, *Failure of World Monetary Reform, 1971–74*, chap. 6. I should note, in this regard, that Chrystal is incorrect when he argues that the optimum-quantity-of-money argument for paying full market rates of interest is irrelevant to SDRs because interest is not paid on the entire level of SDR holdings. Chrystal fails to distinguish between marginal and inframarginal considerations. The fact that interest is paid or received only on deviations between SDR allocations and holdings is an inframarginal consideration that would affect rational economic behavior only through wealth effects. Economically relevant marginal decisions on SDR use do face the opportunity cost of the SDR interest rate, and thus the optimum-quantity-of-money arguments do apply. However, as noted in chapter 2, the simple application of the optimum-quantity-of-money approach should be broadened to take into account the public choice and externality considerations emphasized in Tower and Willett, "More on Official versus Market Financing," pp. 537–52.

There is furthermore an important equity argument for continued SDR creation to reduce the degree of relative disadvantage of those countries that do not have effective access to borrowing from the private international financial markets. One could make a case on similar grounds for an SDR link that would substantially increase the portion of new SDRs allocated to the poorest developing countries. However, my own preference would be to continue instead the recent trend of increasing the access of these countries to special IMF lending facilities.

With respect to the link proposals, there are a number of political and economic arguments both for and against various types of links that I shall not reiterate here.[12] The only point I have to add is that in my judgment both advocates and opponents have exaggerated the effects a link scheme would have. Given the conservative voting structure of the IMF, with an 85 percent weighted vote requirement on SDR creations, it is unlikely that in the foreseeable future even upper-bound estimates on the possibilities of linked SDR creation would have the potential for the magnitude of LDC (less developed country) benefits that many early advocates perceived, or for the inflationary effects opponents feared. The SDR link debate is likely to continue, but its outcome will be of only marginal significance for the operation of the international monetary system.

The Dollar Overhang and Potential Instability from Multiple Reserve Assets

Another issue in which there continues to be a great deal of interest concerns the so-called dollar overhang and the potential instability of a system of multiple reserve assets. Discussion of the dollar overhang often suffers from confusion over a number of different concepts to which this term may refer.[13] In the most popular sense, it often refers to the fact that there are huge quantities of dollars held abroad by both private and official parties. Concerns about these large magnitudes always arise when the outlook for the exchange value of the dollar weakens and funds are shifted out of the dollar into other currencies. Such concerns have given rise to many proposals to "soak up" some of this overhang through unilateral foreign-currency-denominated security issues by the United States or through the

---

[12] For recent discussions of the link proposals, and for references to the vast literature on this subject, see William Cline, *International Monetary Reform and the Developing Countries* (Washington, D.C.: Brookings Institution, 1975); Williamson, "International Liquidity," pp. 685–764; and Williamson, *Failure of World Monetary Reform*, pp. 143–47.
[13] See Willett, *Floating Exchange Rates*, pp. 91–98.

creation of some form of substitution facility by the International Monetary Fund. The latter would deal only with official dollar holdings while the former might be used to attack both sources of potential dollar selling.

Although there are legitimate matters of concern here, advocates of such proposals have often been overly optimistic about the extent to which they could substantially reduce problems of international monetary instability. For example, newspaper reports on proposals for the issuance of foreign currency denominated securities by the United States in exchange for foreign-held dollars often said they were designed to "skim off the speculative froth" against the dollar. But in the face of substantially changed expectations about the outlook for the dollar, it seems quite unlikely that there would be a high degree of correspondence between those most anxious to sell dollars and those who would wish to purchase the new securities. In other words, such security sales would not be a mechanism for fine-tuning the removal of pressures to sell dollars.[14]

Nor is there likely to be a strong relationship between the size of the official or private dollar overhang in a gross sense and the size of the potential exchange market pressures on the dollar. Such pressures result from changes in the outlook for a currency combined with high international capital mobility. Whether the stock of foreign-held dollar-denominated assets at any one time were $200 billion or $400 billion, the potential problem would be the same. Exchange pressure on the dollar can come from U.S. funds moving abroad as well as from selling by foreign dollar holdings. The problems in this area are of high capital mobility in general.

In such an environment, concern about the size of particular figures for various types of foreign-held dollar-denominated balances and efforts to limit their growth are based on a misconception of the basic issues. The fact is that we must either come to terms with living in a world in which, because of high capital mobility, shifts in expectations about the economic outlook for various currencies may have a substantial impact on exchange rates, or we must attempt to establish a very tight and comprehensive system of international regulation and control of both private and official capital flows. In my judgment, the latter approach is unlikely to be either feasible or desirable, but it is the only way to fully insulate reserve currency coun-

[14] The recent official sales of U.S. securities abroad were to purchase foreign currencies for potential use in exchange market intervention, not to soak up foreign dollar holdings. For further discussion, see Thomas D. Willett, "The Fall and Rise of the Dollar" (Testimony before the Subcommittee on International Economics of the Joint Economic Committee, U.S. Congress, December 14, 1978), also available as AEI Reprint No. 96 (Washington, D.C.: American Enterprise Institute, April 1979).

tries and the international monetary system from potential substantial effects from currency switching.[15]

Apart from the question of feasibility, the extent to which one favors continuance of a substantial degree of freedom of capital mobility versus a system of relatively tight control on the economic merits depends largely on how economically rational international capital flows are viewed as being. The development of a relatively high degree of international capital mobility was one of the major factors that led to a breakdown of the Bretton Woods adjustable peg system. Its primary architects, Harry Dexter White of the United States and John Maynard Keynes of the United Kingdom, had been skeptical of the economic desirability of relatively free international capital mobility. They felt that such flows had had a strong tendency to be destabilizing during the economic chaos of the 1930s. They had assumed that the postwar international monetary system would be based on substantial control over capital flows. Subsequent developments and analysis, however, have suggested that Keynes and White were overly optimistic about the extent to which financial capital flows could be controlled without impeding the real side of international economic activity. They also were unduly pessimistic about the degree of economic rationality on which speculative expectations and international capital flows are usually based.

Although such shifts in speculative expectations and international capital flows have often appeared to be extremely disruptive under both the adjustable peg and, to a lesser extent, managed floating, such reactions usually have been well founded. In other words, most of the time private speculations have been more correct than official defenses of exchange rates. The real causes of unsettling exchange market pressures have been the inconsistencies between domestic economic and exchange-rate policies or the instabilities of domestic policies and other underlying economic fundamentals. Capital flows are much like the bearers of bad tidings, who often find themselves blamed for the news they bring.

This is not to say that international capital flows and currency-switching actions are always based on perfectly rational evaluations of the best possible information and forecasts. Nor is it to say that there may not be times in which official intervention in the foreign exchange market is a desirable component of domestic macroecon-

---

[15] The potential magnitude of such a task increases when it is remembered that a substantial portion of exchange-market pressures often comes from defensive shifts caused by hedging and from the timing of commercially related payments, rather than from either the offensive acts of professional currency speculators or the reserve switching of official currency holders.

omic stabilization policies even when speculation is based on reasonable expectations.[16] In my judgment, however, the experiences of the postwar period suggest that economically justifiable cases of heavy official intervention in the exchange markets are the exception rather than the rule. The adoption of floating exchange rates has not eliminated the problem of exchange market instability, but I believe that floating has reduced the extent to which such instability is "artificially" created by international institution arrangements.

The best way to achieve greater stability under floating rates is to evolve more stable underlying economic policies and conditions (particularly in the United States) combined with prudent use of official exchange market intervention within a cooperative international framework, not a system of tight controls over international capital mobility and reserve switching. The latter approach is too blunt. It would be likely to be economically inefficient as well as politically infeasible.

Such a conclusion, of course, does not imply that there may not be net gains possible from the creation of some type of IMF substitution facility to reduce problems of reserve switching. The analysis in this study, however, strongly suggests that such a facility should be viewed as potential marginal improvement, not something which will fill a glaring gap in current international institutional arrangements or make a major contribution to greater international monetary stability.

The traditional distinction between official and private confidence or stability problems was largely a result of the institutional arrangement of the convertibility of officially held currency balances into reserve assets. The abandonment of a general system of reserve asset convertibility and adjustable pegged exchange rates has reduced both the incentives for currency switching in the face of a given economic environment and the degree of distinction between official and private currency holdings. Large exchange-rate changes can still be uncomfortable even under flexible exchange rates. Thus the adoption of floating rates does not completely solve the broad Gresham's-law-type problem of one money driving out another. The potential instability of multiple currencies still remains. It should be remembered, however, that Gresham's law itself was developed in the context of multiple currencies temporarily pegged at disequilibrium exchange rates, an environment that existed under the original Bretton Woods system much more than under the current managed float.

---

[16] For further discussion on these points, see Willett, *Floating Exchange Rates*, chap. 2, and Willett, "International Surveillance of Exchange-Rate Policies," pp.148–72.

Likewise, the factors discussed in chapter 2 that caused the reserve management behavior of the major industrial countries to be much more stabilizing than many expected while the dollar was convertible into gold also suggest that a more general multiple currency system is likely to be less unstable than many have feared. In this respect, the actions of the many smaller official currency holders do not face the same types of restraints as those of the smaller number of large dollar holders. But it is on the behavior of the latter that the stability of the system really depends. They still have the collective power to offset most of the effects of the actions of the former group.

Although the collective international financial power of the traditional large dollar holders has declined in the face of the huge OPEC accumulations, the effective loss of international financial power by this traditional group is really much less than is often supposed. The main alternative outlets for investment still remain within this group of countries, so that currency switches by others will still be predominantly among the currencies of this group rather than into and out of this group of currencies as a whole. Furthermore, the major OPEC currency holders have themselves recognized that they have an increased stake in a relatively smoothly functioning international monetary system and have been relatively conservative with respect to currency switching. Most ditching of the dollar as a result of official portfolio switching has come from the small dollar holders; in aggregate, diversification away from the dollar has not been nearly as great as many popular discussions would seem to imply.[17]

An IMF Substitution Facility

Still, if there were a substantial demand to diversify reserve holdings out of dollars into SDRs, a good case could be made for empowering the IMF to create a facility to issue SDRs in exchange for reserve currency holdings so as to reduce the exchange market pressures resulting from official diversification. A good case can be made for

---

[17] For data and for analysis on this point, see H. Robert Heller and Malcolm Knight, *Reserve Currency Preferences of Central Banks*, Princeton Essays in International Finance, no. 131 (Princeton, N.J.: International Finance Section, Princeton University, 1978), and Leroy Laney, "A Diminished Role for the Dollar as a Reserve Currency?" *Voice of the Federal Reserve Bank of Dallas* (December 1978), pp. 11–23. The proportion of dollars in official currency holdings has fluctuated within a couple of points of 80 percent during the 1970s. For an interesting discussion of central bank practices, see "How Central Banks are Ditching the Dollar," *Euromoney* (October 1978), pp. 31–43, and D. Sykes Wilford and Bluford H. Putnam, "How Diversification Makes the Dollar Weaker," ibid., pp. 201–4.

gold substitution facilities as well.[18] Again it should be remembered that neither reserve currency nor gold substitution facilities would be adequate to generate substantially greater control over international reserve aggregates unless they were made mandatory and were coupled with requirements for asset settlement or some other stringent mechanism. Creation of a higher proportion of SDRs in international liquidity will not in itself do anything substantial to provide greater control of international liquidity.

It should also be recognized that there can be important differences among the types of substitution facilities that could be created and in the treatment of the reserve currencies that they received. One major factor influencing U.S. willingness to favor such a facility would be the obligations placed on IMF holdings of dollars acquired through substitution account operations.

I will not try to go into all of the technical issues involved. These were investigated extensively during the negotiations of the Committee of Twenty and are being investigated again now in detail by the IMF. A few major points should briefly be discussed, however. The issues of convertibility and amortization that figured heavily in the discussions of the Committee of Twenty are of much less relevance today. The question of the terms of U.S. obligation with respect to interest rates and exchange guarantees, if any, continues to be of significant interest, however.

U.S. financial authorities would of course prefer that such obligations bear low interest rates and no exchange guarantee, while the IMF interest would be just the reverse. Obviously a compromise between these extremes should be made. There are two obvious alternatives: (1) The IMF should continue to invest the dollars it acquired in competitive financial instruments in the United States with no exchange-rate guarantee, or (2) the U.S. should issue to the IMF special SDR-denominated securities carrying an interest rate approx-

---

[18] Based on the analysis in chapter 2, I am less concerned about the effects of the current ambiguous role of gold on the operation of the world economy than writers such as David Fand, "World Reserves and World Inflation," Banca Nazionale del Lavoro *Quarterly Review*, no. 115 (December 1975); Fritz Machlup, "Between Outline and Outcome the Reform Was Lost," in E. M. Berstein et al., *Reflections on Jamaica*, Princeton Essays in International Finance, no. 115 (Princeton, N.J.: International Finance Section, Princeton University, 1976); and Williamson in *The Failure of World Monetary Reform*, chap. 6, and in "Techniques to Control International Reserves," pp. 228–30. I do not believe that there is an urgent need to do something about gold. Still, the possibility of creating a gold SDR substitution account is worth consideration. A strong argument against such a facility, however, is that to induce sales, gold conversions would probably have to be valued at close to market rates. There might be scope, however, for further use of profit-sharing principles in the current procedures for IMF gold sales, under which the profits are shared betweeen the original owners and a trust fund that is used to lower the interest payments of low-income countries.

imately equal to the regular SDR interest rate. Given the current formula that sets SDR interest rates at roughly half of major national money market rates, either method would seem to be a reasonable compromise between U.S. and IMF financial interests.

The situation might become more complicated if SDR rates were raised to average market levels, as some have proposed. Then the United States in effect would be giving an exchange guarantee with little corresponding reduction in the interest rate. Still, with good will, working out mutually acceptable financial terms should not be a major stumbling block. Although it would clearly be against narrow U.S. interests to offer an SDR exchange value guarantee on financial instruments that carry normal dollar interest rates, there is no presumption that offering SDR-denominated financial instruments per se would be against longer-term U.S. interests, even narrowly defined.[19]

Possible Types of Substitution Facilities. Such considerations do raise an important issue with respect to the flexibility of the substitution account, however. If the substitution account were freely reversible—that is, if SDRs could be converted back into currencies—it could well contribute to reserve switching by increasing the incentives for the countries to switch out of the dollar when it looked weak

---

[19] Although I think that the United States should not be opposed to an exchange guarantee in principle, I believe that it would be better to have the United States take an above-quota share of the cost of any future liquidation of the facility, rather than having a year-by-year arrangement for compensating for exchange gains and losses.

Payment of interest in dollars with the long-run liquidation commitment would allow one to duck the tricky question of whether an appropriate SDR interest rate on year-by-year SDR-guaranteed dollar holdings should equal the straight weighted average of interest rates for the major SDR currencies, or whether a diversification adjustment should be deducted from this average. Good arguments can be made both for and against such a diversification adjustment (depending largely on whether the relevant alternative is considered to be diversified or only partially diversified official currency holdings). It might be better to avoid having to take a stand on this issue with respect to substitution facility dollar holdings. Of course, the issue cannot be ducked entirely, as it is relevant to the general SDR interest rate. But I think negotiators would be less open to criticism for having made a bad deal on the general interest rate for SDRs than would be the case with SDR-guaranteed dollars.

I would favor having the substitution SDRs be fully, rather than partially, guaranteed in the case of liquidation, with the guarantee being split between the general IMF membership and the United States. With roughly a 20 percent quota, the United States might offer to bear, say, 30 or 40 percent of the guarantee, with the rest being distributed among all other IMF members in proportion to quotas.

For further discussion of these and other substitution account issues, such as acceptance limits and designation procedures, see Morgan Guaranty Trust, "Reserve Diversification and the IMF Substitution Account," *World Financial Markets* (September 1979), pp. 5–14, and Dorothy M. Sobol, "A Substitution Account: Precedence and Issues," Federal Reserve Bank of New York *Quarterly Review*, vol. 4, no. 2 (Summer 1979), pp. 40–48.

and into the dollar when it looked strong. The substitution account would minimize the exchange-rate effects of reserve switching. But by this very result it would increase the incentives of national reserve managers to play the market in effect at the expense of the United States and/or the IMF, depending on the particular financial arrangements concerning dollars acquired by the IMF through the substitution facility.

As a consequence, one suggestion would be that any IMF substitution facility not be freely reversible.[20] SDRs would not be convertible back into currencies except for balance-of-payments needs. This would maintain the original philosophy that SDRs not be sold for the purpose of switching reserve composition. I see no objection, however, to allowing as an exception mutually agreeable transfer of SDRs and currencies among individual financial authorities.

A remaining question is whether a substitution account should be once and for all or open ended. There are some merits on both sides. An open-ended account would be likely to "subsidize" to some extent official speculation at the expense of the United States and/or the IMF, although not nearly to the degree of a reversible substitution account. On the other hand, a one-time consolidation could satisfy only present and not future demands for diversification. It should also be recognized that because the SDR is not the only asset countries might want to diversify into, the total reduction in the desire to diversify out of dollars would be expected to be less than the demand to diversify into SDRs. Such a facility could not eliminate, even for a particular time, all potential desires to diversify from one currency to another.

The creation of a new SDR facility might make new dollar accumulations more onerous to the United States. This could happen because of conversion into SDRs on unfavorable financial terms to the United States or because of potentially more stringent convertibility obligations if some of the old Committee of Twenty proposals

---

[20] This concept of a new IMF facility would make it like the mechanisms for consolidation discussed during the Committee of Twenty negotiations, rather than like the substitution facilities that were often envisioned as mandatory, and that in some versions had one objective of providing a buffer for asset convertibility with respect to the United States; that is, countries would be required to convert dollar accumulations into SDRs, but under some circumstances the IMF would not convert these dollars into U.S.-owned reserve assets, thus providing a form of elasticity alternative to the U.S. reserve indicator proposals. For further discussion, see Williamson, *Failure of World Monetary Reform.* Following recent convention, however, I shall continue to refer to the whole set of possible new facilities as substitution accounts. For further discussion, see William Fellner, "The Dollar's Place in the International System," *Journal of Economic Literature,* vol. 10, no. 3 (September 1972), pp. 735–56; Peter B. Kenen, "Convertibility and Consolidation: A Survey of Options for Reform," *American Economic Review,* vol. 63, no. 2 (May 1973), pp. 189–98; and Williamson, *Failure of World Monetary Reform.*

were adopted in some future round of international monetary negotiations. New dollar accumulations might be more advantageous to the holders. To the extent that such accumulations had these results, there should be assurances that such accumulations took place with the blessing of the United States, or within an internationally agreed-upon framework, or both. It would hardly be equitable or efficient to provide in effect a "subsidy" through an IMF facility to a country accumulating dollars as a result of maintaining an undervalued currency against the wishes of the United States and the IMF.

Linking Access to the Substitution Facility to International Surveillance of the Adjustment Process. Perhaps the most desirable approach would be to establish an open-ended but nonreversible substitution facility, and to strengthen the arrangements for IMF surveillance of the adjustment process so that only currencies accumulated by actions sanctioned by (or at a minimum not discouraged by) the IMF for surveillance would be eligible for substitution.

Probably the best way to structure such an approach would be to allow access to the substitution facility only to countries judged to be meeting the IMF guidelines. Although this leaves the problem of how to treat a country that has violated the guidelines but has come back into compliance, this seems a more feasible approach than trying to distinguish between the portions of a country's currency holdings that were and were not eligible for substitution. Furthermore, prohibitions on conversions of the latter would not begin to have any real effect until all eligible currency holdings had already been converted.

One possibility would be to bar a country's access to the facility while it was in violation of the guidelines and for some specified time after it again met the guidelines. The length of additional ineligibility could vary with the severity of the violation. This system could be combined with limitations on the total amount of currency that could be converted, calculated in such a way that the total amount a country could convert could not be increased by accumulations taking place outside of the guidelines. There would be a number of technical complications involved in such an approach that would need careful study. It might nevertheless offer an attractive method both of improving international surveillance of the adjustment process and of reducing some of the strains that would be caused by increased desires for currency diversification over time.

By requiring judgments on the consistency of a country's behavior with the IMF guidelines for exchange-rate and balance-of-payments surveillance, this approach might add a useful degree of formalism and importance to the international surveillance process, without the disadvantage of the old scarce-currency-clause provisions for trade sanctions that were so severe that they were never used. This approach is similar in spirit to earlier proposals for graduated financial penalties on countries violating agreed-upon adjustment standards. Such an idea was included among Keynes's original proposals at Bretton Woods, and was discussed during the Committee of Twenty negotiations. Although the direct economic cost implied by the types of penalties discussed—for example, reduction in interest paid on SDR holdings—would not be great, such prospective penalties might be an important component of international moral suasion.

It can be argued that given the difficulties of determining good behavior precisely, it would be inadvisable to deal with surveillance and SDR conversion issues in a highly formal manner with the periodic public classification of all countries into those that are and those that are not conforming to the guidelines. Acceptance of such a view (to which I am quite sympathetic) does not undercut the case for linking surveillance to SDR conversion, however. These could be linked in a looser fashion along the following lines. There would be an initial conversion open to all. (I would not place limits on the amounts that countries could initially convert.) Future use of the facility would require IMF approval, with the approval depending in part on reasonable conformity with the surveillance rules. In questionable cases, a country could quietly seek a view as to whether they were in conformity or not. They could be given an initial view that could indicate whether there would be problems. The country could then decide whether it wished to run the risk of a turndown of a formal proposal.

Although there would be numerous practical issues in implementing this approach, it would allow a much more effective facility than alternatives relying only on periodic open days, say once a year, for conversions after the initial round. In the absence of some linkage to international surveillance of exchange-rate policies and the adjustment process, perhaps only a one-time consolidation is all that would be justified.

Of course, neither a one-time nor an open-ended nonreversible substitution facility would solve the problem of potential currency instability. This objective requires sound domestic economic policies and the wise use of official intervention in exchange markets in particular instances. As long as there is substantial international capital mobility, the potential for large exchange-rate fluctuations will exist. Properly designed, however, an SDR substitution facility could make

99

a useful marginal contribution by reducing the exchange market pressures resulting from official desires to achieve greater diversification of reserve holdings.

Strengthening the Role of the IMF

No international monetary system will work well if the underlying economic and financial conditions in the major countries are not relatively stable. International monetary institutions and operating principles are important, however, as the adverse consequences of the breakdown of the Bretton Woods system clearly indicated. Although I have argued that the resulting international liquidity explosion did not contribute as much to the subsequent worldwide inflation as many have assumed, these adverse effects were certainly not trivial.

The effects of international liquidity increases depend importantly on their causes, however, and the shift to more flexible exchange rates has done a great deal to shield countries from undesired international liquidity creation. This study suggests that our new international monetary system is likely to be much more durable than many critics have feared, but exchange-rate flexibility is not a complete solution to international monetary problems. Although countries can now shield themselves much better from inflationary developments abroad, there is still considerable scope under managed floating for countries to export inflationary or deflationary pressures to others.

There are likewise times in which official financing of payments deficits may be in the interests of the international community. There is no clear-cut set of quantitative criteria, however, to determine when official balance-of-payments financing is desirable and when it is not. Although the use of many types of technical quantitative analysis can be extremely useful, we must ultimately rely on careful case-by-case judgments of when financing is desirable. Given my belief that flexible exchange rates have worked relatively well, this suggests that the International Monetary Fund should be given a much stronger role in deciding when heavy official intervention and balance-of-payments financing is internationally acceptable.

This role should include surveillance over official borrowing from the private international financial markets. At the same time, the IMF should be able to provide discretionary financing as needed to offset or reduce the effects of international monetary instabilities that may occur and to sanction and finance the international component of internationally approved national stabilization policies.[21]

---

[21] For a recent discussion of IMF lending facilities and policies, see Andrew D. Crockett and H. Robert Heller, "The Changing Role of the International Monetary Fund," *Kredit und Kapital*, Heft 3 (1978), pp. 324–39.

As was noted above, I believe that there is a good case for continued SDR allocations under the present system of managed flexibility of exchange rates. With greater exchange-rate flexibility, however, there is a much weaker case for automatically financing incipient payments deficits. Much greater discretion should be utilized for reserve use under managed floating, and there should be much closer international surveillance over the early stages of reserve use under managed floating than under the adjustable peg system. In such circumstances, it would seem wise to tilt the mix of owned reserves and conditionally available credit in the direction of the latter. Such a tilt would give greater weight to the need to secure international agreement that instances of substantial official intervention were justified, or at least were not of the beggar-thy-neighbor variety.

Strengthening of the surveillance and conditional liquidity operations of the IMF—not grand designs to return to asset settlement and quantitative control of international liquidity aggregates—is the most feasible and effective way of providing better management of international liquidity and of the operation of the international monetary system. In the process it could prove desirable to create a new IMF substitution facility, but such a facility would need to be carefully designed, and should be linked to the international surveillance of exchange-rate policies and the adjustment process.

4

Summary and Conclusions

This study has sought to present a framework for viewing the role of international liquidity developments in the operation of the international monetary system, and to use this framework to present an analytic history of major international liquidity developments and to analyze a number of current policy issues. The following points summarize some of the major conclusions.

1. In analyzing international liquidity, confidence, and adjustment problems, it is important to take into account the bureaucratic and political incentives facing decision makers as well as strictly economic considerations.

2. There is not a sufficiently strong and systematic relationship between reserve changes and national economic behavior to use the behavior of international reserve aggregates as a guide to international liquidity policies in the way that the behavior of national monetary aggregates can be used as a guide to national monetary policy. The causes of reserve changes and their distribution among countries have a major impact on their effects.

3. The most promising way to improve the operation of the international monetary aspects of the world economy is through focusing directly on the operation of the international adjustment process. Attempts to control international liquidity aggregates through a return to convertibility of currencies into reserve assets or the establishment of mandatory asset settlement through the International Monetary Fund are likely to be less effective than the continuation of flexible exchange rates combined with strengthened international surveillance of national exchange-rate and balance-of-payments adjustment and financing policies. Such surveillance should include oversight of official borrowing from the private financial markets.

4. Although the international liquidity explosion of 1970–1972

did have a significant impact on the acceleration of worldwide inflation, this effect was not nearly as large as many have argued. It was
a consequence of the breakdown of the old pegged exchange-rate
system rather than of the new international monetary system based
on more flexible exchange rates. Managed floating does not offer a
complete cure for the traditional international liquidity and confidence problems of the old pegged-rate system, but it has greatly
reduced the magnitude of these problems.

5. The current loosely structured international monetary system
does not present a neat blueprint for handling international monetary
problems, but it requires much less sacrifice of national sovereignty
than proposals for highly structured reforms of the international
monetary system. Although it probably would be desirable for countries to accept a greater degree of international control over their
international financial policies to reduce potential international monetary instabilities, the current international monetary arrangements
appear to be much more durable than many critics have feared.

6. Uncontrolled expansion of the Eurocurrency markets and official borrowing from private international financial markets have not
been as serious a cause of global inflation and escape from international financial discipline as many have feared. Nor has the existence
of multiple official reserve assets led to the degree of international
monetary instability that some have predicted. Currency switching
by the oil-exporting countries has not been one of the most important
causes of exchange-rate fluctuations. Had their large financial accumulations been accomplished primarily by a redistribution rather than
by an expansion of international liquidity, there would have been a
substantial risk that the oil shock would have generated a much more
severe worldwide recession and stimulated economic warfare remi-
niscent of the 1930s.

7. The potential problems usually associated with "uncontrolled"
international liquidity creation and currency switching will not be
substantially cured by relatively mild measures such as the placement
of reserve requirements on the Eurocurrency markets or the creation
of an IMF substitution facility to acquire unwanted dollar holdings.
The most serious problems associated with all of these phenomena
come from the existence of high international capital mobility combined with instabilities in underlying economic and financial conditions. To improve international monetary stability, either the stability
of underlying conditions and policies must be increased, or comprehensive regulation of private and official international capital flows
will be required. There is, of course, considerable question about both
the feasibility and desirability of the latter approach.

8. A modest rate of SDR creation should be continued, but greater emphasis should be placed on strengthening the resources of the IMF for discretionary lending in cases in which substantial official exchange market intervention is deemed to be in the international interest. Although official demands for international reserve holdings are likely to continue to grow over time and should be met largely by increases in SDRs rather than national currency holdings, the adoption of managed floating greatly increases the judgmental element in deciding when reserve use is desirable and when not. The most important contributions to reducing international monetary instability will come not from formal reform of our international monetary procedures and institutions but from the adoption of more stable national economic and financial policies and continued strengthening of the basic fabric of international economic cooperation. The United States has a particularly strong responsibility in this regard.

Although an IMF substitution facility is not likely to make a major contribution to enhancing international monetary stability, such a facility could be well worthwhile if appropriately designed and linked to provisions for international surveillance of the adjustment process.

Bibliography

Ahtiala, Pekka. "Monetary Policy in National and International Economics." In *International Reserves: Needs and Availability*. Washington, D.C.: International Monetary Fund, 1970.

Amacher, Ryan C.; Tollison, Robert D.; and Willett, Thomas D. "Risk Avoidance and Political Advertising: Neglected Issues in the Literature on Budget Size in a Democracy." In *The Economic Approach to Public Policy*, edited by Amacher, Tollison, and Willett. Ithaca, N.Y.: Cornell University Press, 1976.

———. "The Divergence between (Trade) Theory and Practice." In Walter Adams et al. *Tariffs, Quotas, and Trade: The Politics of Protectionism*. San Francisco, Calif.: Institute for Contemporary Studies, 1979.

Argy, Victor, and Kouri, Penti. "Sterilization Policies and the Volatility in International Reserves." In *National Monetary Policies and the International Financial System*, edited by Robert Z. Aliber. Chicago, Ill.: University of Chicago Press, 1974.

Artus, Jacques. "Exchange Rate Stability and Managed Floating: The Experience of the Federal Republic of Germany." *IMF Staff Papers* 23 (July 1976): 312–33.

Basevi, Giorgio. "Review of Floating Exchange Rates and International Monetary Reform." *Journal of International Economics* 9 (February 1979): 143–46.

Bilson, John F. O., and Frenkel, Jacob A. "Dynamic Adjustment and the Demand for International Reserves." International Economics Workshop Report No. 7942. Chicago, Ill.: Department of Economics, University of Chicago, 1979.

Bloomfield, A. I. *Monetary Policy under the International Gold Standard: 1880–1914*. New York: Federal Reserve Board, 1959.

Buchanan, James M., and Wagner, Richard. *Democracy in Deficit*. New York: Academic Press, 1977.

105

Carli, Guido, et al. "A Debate on the Eurodollar Market." *Quaderni di Ricerche.* Ente per gli studi monetari, bancari e finanziari "Luigi Einaudi," no. 11 (1972).

Chrystal, K. Alec. *International Money and the Future of the SDR.* Princeton Essays in International Finance, no. 128. Princeton, N.J.: International Finance Section, Princeton University, 1978.

Clark, Peter B. "Demand for International Reserves: A Cross-Country Analysis." *Canadian Journal of Economics* 3 (November 1970): 577–94.

———. "Optimum International Reserves and the Speed of Adjustment." *Journal of Political Economy* 78 (March/April 1970): 356–76.

Cline, William. *International Monetary Reform and the Developing Countries.* Washington, D.C.: Brookings Institution, 1975.

Cohen, Benjamin J. "International Reserves and Liquidity." In *International Trade and Finance,* edited by Peter B. Kenen. Cambridge, England: Cambridge University Press, 1975.

———. *Organizing the World's Money: The Political Economy of International Monetary Relations.* New York: Basic Books, 1977.

Cohen, Stephen D. *International Monetary Reform, 1964–69: The Political Dimension.* New York: Praeger, 1970.

Cooper, Richard N. *Currency Devaluation in Developing Countries.* Princeton Essays in International Finance, no. 86. Princeton, N.J.: International Finance Section, Princeton University, 1971.

———. "International Liquidity and Balance of Payments Adjustment." In *International Reserves: Needs and Availability.* Washington, D.C.: International Monetary Fund, 1970.

———. "Monetary Theory and Policy in an Open Economy." *Scandinavian Journal of Economics* 78 (1976): 146–65.

———. "Prolegomena to the Choice of an International Monetary System." In *World Politics and International Economics,* edited by C. Fred Bergsten and L. B. Krause. Washington, D.C.: Brookings Institution, 1975.

Corden, W. M. *Inflation, Exchange Rates, and the World Economy.* Chicago, Ill.: University of Chicago Press, 1977.

Crockett, Andrew D. "Control over International Reserves." *IMF Staff Papers,* vol. 25, no. 1. Washington, D.C.: International Monetary Fund, 1978.

———. "The Eurocurrency Market: An Attempt to Clarify Some Basic Issues." *IMF Staff Papers,* vol. 23, no. 2. Washington, D.C.: International Monetary Fund, 1976.

———, and Goldstein, Morris. "Inflation under Fixed and Flexible Exchange Rates." *IMF Staff Papers,* vol. 23, no. 3. Washington, D.C.: International Monetary Fund, 1976.

———, and Heller, H. Robert. "The Changing Role of the International Monetary Fund." *Kredit und Kapital,* Heft 3 (1978): 324–39.

Depres, Emile; Kindleberger, Charles P.; and Salant, Walter S. "The Dollar and World Liquidity: A Minority View." *The Economist* 218 (February 1966): 526–29.

106

de Vries, Tom. "Jamaica, or the Non-Reform of the International Monetary System." *Foreign Affairs* 54 (April 1976): 577–605.

Dreyer, Jacob. *Composite Reserve Assets in the International Monetary System.* Greenwich, Conn.: JAI Press, 1977.

———; Haberler, Gottfried; and Willett, Thomas D.; eds. *Exchange-Rate Flexibility.* Washington, D.C.: American Enterprise Institute, 1978.

Dufey, Gunter, and Giddy, Ian H. *The International Money Market.* Englewood Cliffs, N.J.: Prentice Hall, 1978.

Dutton, John. "Effective Protection, Taxes on Foreign Investment, and the Operation of the Gold Standard." Ph.D. dissertation, Duke University, 1978.

Fand, David. "World Reserves and World Inflation." Banca Nazionale del Lavoro *Quarterly Review,* no. 115 (December 1975).

Fellner, William. "The Dollar's Place in the International System." *Journal of Economic Literature* 10 (September 1972): 735–56.

Frenkel, Jacob A. "International Reserves, Pegged Exchange Rates, and Managed Floating." In *Economic Policies in Open Economics,* edited by Karl Brunner and Allan H. Meltzer. Carnegie-Rochester Conference Series on Public Policy, vol. 9. A Supplementary Series to the *Journal of Monetary Economics* (1978).

———. "International Reserves under Pegged Exchange Rates and Managed Float: Corrections and Extensions." Working Paper. Chicago, Ill.: Department of Economics, University of Chicago, 1979.

———, and Jovanovic, Boyan. "Optimal International Reserves: A Stochastic Framework." International Economics Workshop Working Paper. Chicago, Ill.: Department of Economics, University of Chicago, 1979.

Frey, Burro S. "Politico-Economic Models and Cycles." *Journal of Public Economics* 9 (April 1978): 203–20.

Goldstein, Henry. "Monetary Policy under Fixed and Floating Rates." National Westminster Bank *Quarterly Review* (November 1974): 15–27.

Gordon, Robert J. "The Demand and Supply of Inflation." *Journal of Law and Economics* 18 (December 1975): 807–36.

Grubel, Herbert G. "International Monetarism and World Inflation." *Weltwirtschaftliches Archiv,* Heft 1 (1978).

———. "The Demand for International Reserves: A Critical Review of the Literature." *Journal of Economic Literature* 9 (December 1971): 1148–66.

Haberler, Gottfried. "How Important Is Control over International Reserves?" In *The New International Monetary System,* edited by Robert Mundell and Jacques J. Polak. New York: Columbia University Press, 1977.

———, and Willett, Thomas D. *U.S. Balance of Payments Policies and International Monetary Reform.* Washington, D.C.: American Enterprise Institute, 1968.

Harrod, Roy. *Reforming the World's Money.* London: Macmillan, 1965.

Heller, H. Robert. "Further Evidence on the Relationship between International Reserves and World Inflation." Mimeographed. International Monetary Fund, 1977.

―――. "International Reserves and Worldwide Inflation." *IMF Staff Papers*, vol. 23, no. 1. Washington, D.C.: International Monetary Fund, 1976.

―――, and Khan, Moskin S. "The Demand for International Reserves under Fixed and Flexible Exchange Rates." *IMF Staff Papers*, vol. 25, no. 4. Washington, D.C.: International Monetary Fund, 1978.

―――, and Knight, Malcolm. *Reserve Currency Preferences of Central Banks*. Princeton Essays in International Finance, no. 131. Princeton, N.J.: International Finance Section, Princeton University, 1978.

Herring, Richard J., and Marston, Richard C. *National Monetary Policies and International Finance Markets*. Amsterdam: North Holland, 1977.

―――. "Sterilization Policy." *European Economic Review* (December 1977).

Hewson, John, and Sakakibara, Eisuke. "The Euro-Dollar Multiplier: A Portfolio Approach." *IMF Staff Papers*, vol. 21, no. 2. Washington, D.C.: International Monetary Fund, 1974.

Hickman, B.G., and Schleicher, S. "The Interdependence of National Economies and the Synchronization of Economic Fluctuations: Evidence from the Link Project." *Weltwirtschaftliches Archiv*, Heft 4 (1978).

Hipple, F. Steb. *The Disturbances Approach to the Demand for International Reserves*. Princeton Studies in International Finance, no. 35. Princeton, N.J.: International Finance Section, Princeton University, 1974.

Hirsch, Fred. *An SDR Standard: Impetus, Elements, and Impediments*. Princeton Essays in International Finance, no. 99. Princeton, N.J.: International Finance Section, Princeton University, 1973.

―――. "SDRs and the Working of the Gold Exchange Standard. *IMF Staff Papers*, vol. 18, no. 2. Washington, D.C.: International Monetary Fund, 1971.

―――; Doyle, Michael; and Morse, Edward L. *Alternatives to Monetary Disorder*. New York: McGraw-Hill, 1977.

―――, and Goldthorpe, John H., eds. *The Political Economy of Inflation*. Cambridge, Mass.: Harvard University Press, 1978.

"How Central Banks are Ditching the Dollar." *Euromoney* (October 1978): 31–43.

International Monetary Fund. "The Fund under the Second Amendment: A Supplement." *IMF Survey*. September 18, 1978.

Johnson, Harry G. "International Liquidity and Balance of Payments: Comment." In *International Reserves: Needs and Availability*. Washington, D.C.: International Monetary Fund, 1970.

Katz, Samuel I. *External Surpluses, Capital Flows, and Credit Policy in the European Economic Community*. Princeton Studies in International Finance, no. 22. Princeton, N.J.: International Finance Section, Princeton University, 1969.

Kelly, Michael G. "The Demand for International Reserves." *American Economic Review* 60 (September 1970): 655–67.

Kenen, Peter B. "Convertibility and Consolidation: A Survey of Options for Reform." *American Economic Review* 63 (May 1973): 189–98.

―――. "Techniques to Control International Reserves." In *The New Inter-*

national Monetary System, edited by Robert Mundell and Jacques J. Polak. New York: Columbia University Press, 1977.

Keran, Michael K. "Towards an Explanation of Simultaneous Inflation-Recession." San Francisco Federal Reserve Bank *Business Review* (Spring 1975): 18–30.

Kreinin, Mordechai, and Officer, Lawrence H. *The Monetary Approach to the Balance of Payments: A Survey*. Princeton Studies in International Finance, no. 43. Princeton, N.J.: International Finance Section, Princeton University, 1978.

Laney, Leroy. "A Diminished Role for the Dollar as a Reserve Currency?" *Voice of the Federal Reserve Bank of Dallas* (December 1978): 11–23.

————. "National Monetary Independence and Managed Floating Exchange Rates." Paper presented to Federal Reserve System Committee on International Research and Analysis, Boston, October 1978. Unpublished.

————, and Willett, Thomas D. "The International Liquidity Explosion and Worldwide Monetary Expansion: 1970–1972." Claremont Working Papers. Claremont, Calif.: Claremont Graduate School, 1980.

————. *The Political Economy of Global Inflation: The Causes of Monetary Expansion in the Major Industrial Countries*. Washington, D.C.: American Enterprise Institute, forthcoming.

————. "United States Monetary Policy and the Political Business Cycle." Claremont Working Papers. Claremont, Calif.: Claremont Graduate School, 1980.

Little, Jane S. "Liquidity Creation by Euro-banks: 1973–1978." *New England Economic Review* (January/February 1979): 62–72.

Logue, Dennis; Sweeney, Richard; and Willett, Thomas D. "The Speculative Behavior of Exchange Rates during the Current Float." *Journal of Business Research* 6 (May 1978): 159–74.

McCloskey, D. N., and Zecher, J. R. "How the Gold Standard Worked, 1880–1913." In *The Monetary Approach to the Balance of Payments*, edited by J. A. Frenkel and H. G. Johnson. London: Allen and Unwin, 1976.

Machlup, Fritz. "Between Outline and Outcome the Reform Was Lost." In E. M. Berstein et al. *Reflections on Jamaica*. Princeton Essays in International Finance, no. 115. Princeton, N.J.: International Finance Section, Princeton University, 1976.

————. "Further Reflections on the Demand for Foreign Reserves." In *International Payments, Debts, and Gold*, edited by Fritz Machlup. New York: Charles Scribner's Sons, 1964.

————. *Remaking the International Monetary System*. Baltimore, Md.: Johns Hopkins University Press, 1968.

————. "The Need for Monetary Reserves." Banca Nazionale del Lavoro *Quarterly Review*, no. 78 (September 1966): 175–222.

McKinnon, Ronald I. "Review of Floating Exchange Rates and International Monetary Reform." *Journal of Economic Literature* 16 (December 1978): 1469–73.

————. *The Eurocurrency Market*. Princeton Essays in International Finance, no. 125. Princeton, N.J.: International Finance Section, Princeton University, 1977.

Mahar, K. L., and Porter, M. G.. "International Reserves and Capital Mobility." In *The Political Economy of Monetary Reform*, edited by Robert Z. Aliber. Montclair, N.J.: Allanheld, Osmun and Co., 1977.

Makin, John H. "Exchange Rate Flexibility and the Demand for International Reserves." *Weltwirtschaftliches Archiv*, Heft 2 (1974): 229–42.

———. "On the Success of the Reserve Currency System in the Crisis Zone." *Journal of International Economics* 2 (February 1972): 77–85.

———. "Reserve Adequacy before and after Limited Floating." *Journal of Economics and Business* 30 (Fall 1977): 8–14.

Mayer, Helmut W. *Some Theoretical Problems Relating to the Euro-Dollar Market*. Princeton Essays in International Finance, no. 79. Princeton, N.J.: International Finance Section, Princeton University, 1970.

———. "The BIS Concept of the Eurocurrency Market." *Euromoney* (May 1976): 60–66.

Mayer, Martin. "The Incredible Shrinking Dollar." *The Atlantic Monthly* 242 (August 1978): 59–65.

Meiselman, D. I. "Worldwide Inflation: A Monetarist View." In *The Phenomenon of Worldwide Inflation*, edited by D. I. Meiselman and A. B. Laffer. Washington: American Enterprise Institute, 1975.

Michaely, Michael. *Balance-of-Payments Adjustment Policies: Japan, Germany, and the Netherlands*. National Bureau of Economic Research Occasional Paper No. 106. New York: National Bureau of Economic Research, 1968.

Miller, N. D. "Sterilization and Offset Coefficients for Five Industrial Countries and the Monetary Approach to the Balance of Payments." Mimeographed. Pittsburgh, Penn.: Department of Economics, University of Pittsburgh.

Morgan Guaranty Trust. "Reserve Diversification and the IMF Substitution Account." *World Financial Markets* (September 1979): 5–14.

———. "The Eurocurrency Market." *World Financial Markets* (January 1979): 9–14.

Mueller, Dennis C. *Public Choice*. Cambridge, England: Cambridge University Press, 1979.

Mundell, Robert. "The International Disequilibrium System." *Kyklos*, fasc. 2 (1961): 153–72.

———. "The Optimum Balance of Payments Deficit." In *Stabilization Policies in Interdependence Economics*, edited by Emile Classen and Pascal Salin. London: North Holland, 1972.

———, and Polak, Jacques J., eds. *The New International Monetary System*. New York: Columbia University Press, 1977.

Murphy, J. Carter. "SDRs, Dollars, and Other International Reserves." Paper presented at the meeting of the Southwest Social Science Association, Fort Worth, Texas, March 30, 1979.

———. *The International Monetary System*. Washington, D.C.: American Enterprise Institute, 1979.

Niehans, Jürg. "The Need for Reserves of a Single Country." In *International Reserves: Needs and Availability*. Washington, D.C.: International Monetary Fund, 1970.

———, and Hewson, John. "The Eurocurrency Market and Monetary Theory." *Journal of Money, Credit, and Banking* 8 (February 1976): 1–29.

Nordhaus, W. D. "The Political Business Cycle." *Review of Economic Studies* 42 (April 1975): 169–90.

Officer, Lawrence H. "Reserve-Asset Preferences in the Crisis Zone, 1958–67." *Journal of Money, Credit, and Banking* 6 (May 1974): 191–213.

———. "The Purchasing Power Parity Theory of Exchange Rates: A Review Article." *IMF Staff Papers*, vol. 23, no. 1. Washington, D.C.: International Monetary Fund, 1976.

———, and Willett, Thomas D. "Reserve-Asset Preferences and the Confidence Problem in the Crisis Zone." *Quarterly Journal of Economics* 83 (November 1969): 688–95.

———. "The Interaction of Adjustment and Gold Conversion Policies in a Reserve-Currency System." *Western Economic Journal* 8 (March 1970): 47–60.

Organization for Economic Cooperation and Development. *OECD Outlook* (July 1978).

Ossola, R. "Central Bank Intervention and Eurocurrency Markets." Banca Nazionale del Lavoro *Quarterly Review*, no. 104 (March 1973): 29–45.

Polak, Jacques. "Money: National and International." In *International Reserves: Needs and Availability*. Washington, D.C.: International Monetary Fund, 1970.

———. *Valuation and Rate of Interest of the SDR*. Washington, D.C.: International Monetary Fund, 1974.

Salant, Walter S. "Practical Techniques for Assessing the Need for World Reserves." In *International Reserves: Needs and Availability*. Washington, D.C.: International Monetary Fund, 1970.

Sammons, Robert L. "International Debt: Its Growth and Significance." Study prepared for the Special Study on Economic Change of the Joint Economic Committee, U.S. Congress, 1979.

Savona, Paola. "Controlling the Euromarkets." Banca Nazionale del Lavoro *Quarterly Review*, no. 109 (June 1974): 167–74.

Slighton, Robert. "International Liquidity Issues under Flexible Exchange Rates." In *Exchange-Rate Flexibility*, edited by Jacob Dreyer, Gottfried Haberler, and Thomas D. Willett. Washington, D.C.: American Enterprise Institute, 1978.

Sobol, Dorothy M. "A Substitution Account: Precedence and Issues." Federal Reserve Bank of New York *Quarterly Review* 4 (Summer 1979): 40–48.

Sohmen, Egon. "International Liquidity Issues: Discussion." In *Exchange-Rate Flexibility*, edited by Jacob Dreyer, Gottfried Haberler, and Thomas D. Willett. Washington, D.C.: American Enterprise Institute, 1978.

Solomon, Robert. "Techniques to Control International Reserves." In *The New International Monetary System*, edited by Robert Mundell and Jacques J. Polak. New York: Columbia University Press, 1977.

————. "The Allocation of 'Oil Deficits.'" *Brookings Papers on Economic Activity*, no. 1. Washington, D.C.: Brookings Institution, 1975.

————. *The International Monetary System*. New York: Harper and Row, 1977.

Stem, Carl; Logue, Dennis; and Makin, John; eds. *Eurocurrencies and the International Monetary System*. Washington, D.C.: American Enterprise Institute, 1976.

Strange, Susan. *International Monetary Relations*. London: Oxford University Press, 1976.

Suss, Ester. "A Note on Reserve Use under Alternative Exchange Rate Regimes." *IMF Staff Papers*, vol. 23, no. 2. Princeton, N.J.: International Finance Section, Princeton University, 1976.

Sweeney, Richard J., and Willett, Thomas D. "Eurodollars, Petrodollars, and Problems of World Liquidity and Inflation." In *Stabilization of the Domestic and International Economy*, edited by Karl Brunner and Allan H. Meltzer. Carnegie-Rochester Conference Series on Public Policy, vol. 5. A Supplementary Series to the *Journal of Monetary Economics* (1977): 277–310.

————. *Studies on Exchange Rate Flexibility*. Washington, D.C.: American Enterprise Institute, forthcoming.

————. "The International Transmission of Inflation." In *Bank Credit, Money, and Inflation in Open Economies*, edited by Michele Fratianni and Karel Tavevnier. A Special Supplement to *Kredit und Kapital*, Heft 3 (1976): 441–517.

Throop, Adrian W. "Eurobanking and World Inflation." *Voice of the Federal Reserve Bank of Dallas* (August 1979): 8–23.

Thursby, Marie, and Willett, Thomas D. "The Effects of Flexible Exchange Rates on International Trade and Investment." Mimeographed. Claremont, Calif.: Claremont Graduate School, 1980. Forthcoming in *Studies on Exchange Rate Flexibility*, edited by Richard J. Sweeney and Thomas D. Willett. Washington, D.C.: American Enterprise Institute.

Tower, Edward, and Willett, Thomas D. "More on Official versus Market Financing of Payments Deficits and the Optimal Pricing of International Reserves." *Kyklos*, fasc. 3 (1972): 537–52.

————. "The Theory of Optimum Currency Areas and Exchange Rate Flexibility." Special Papers in International Economics, no. 11. Princeton, N.J.: International Finance Section, Princeton University, 1976.

Triffin, Robert. *Gold and the Dollar Crisis*. New Haven, Conn.: Yale University Press, 1960.

————. *Gold and the Dollar Crisis*. Princeton Essays in International Finance, no. 132. Princeton, N.J.: International Finance Section, Princeton University, 1978.

Wallich, Henry C. "Statement on the Eurocurrency Markets," and accompanying "Discussion Paper Concerning Reserve Requirements on Eurocurrency Deposits" by the Federal Reserve Board staff. Presented to the Subcommittee on Domestic Monetary Policy and the Subcommittee on International Trade, Investment, and Monetary Policy of the Committee on Banking, Finance, and Urban Affairs, U.S. House of Representatives, U.S. Congress, July 12, 1979.

Whitman, Marina. "Global Monetarism and the Monetary Approach to the Balance of Payments." In *Brookings Papers on Economic Activity*, no. 3. Washington, D.C.: Brookings Institution, 1975.

———. "Techniques to Control International Reserves: Comment." In *The New International Monetary System*, edited by Robert Mundell and Jacques J. Polak. New York: Columbia University Press, 1977.

Wilford, D. Sykes and Putnam, Bluford H. "How Diversification Makes the Dollar Weaker." *Euromoney* (October 1978): 201–4.

Willett, Thomas D. "Alternative Approaches to International Surveillance of Exchange-Rate Policies." In *Managed Exchange-Rate Flexibility*. Proceedings of a conference sponsored by the Federal Reserve Bank of Boston, October 1978.

———. *Floating Exchange Rates and International Monetary Reform*. Washington, D.C.: American Enterprise Institute, 1977.

———. "It's Too Easy to Blame the Speculators." *Euromoney* (May 1979): 111–20.

———. "It's Too Simple to Blame the Countries with a Surplus." *Euromoney* (February 1978): 89–96.

———. "Official versus Market Financing of International Deficits." *Kyklos*, facs. 3 (1968): 514–24.

———. "Some Aspects of the Public Choice Approach to International Economic Relations." Paper presented at the European University Institute Conference on New Economic Approaches to the Study of International Integration, Florence, Italy, May 31–June 2, 1979. Forthcoming in conference volume to be edited by Pierre Salmon.

———. "The Adequacy of International Means of Payment." *Review of Economics and Statistics* 51 (August 1969): 373–74.

———. "The Eurocurrency Market, Exchange-Rate Systems, and National Financial Policies." In *Eurocurrencies and the International Monetary System*, edited by Carl Stem, Dennis Logue, and John Makin. Washington, D.C.: American Enterprise Institute, 1976.

———. "The Fall and Rise of the Dollar." Testimony before the Subcommittee on International Economics of the Joint Economic Committee, U.S. Congress, December 14, 1978. Also available as AEI Reprint No. 96. Washington, D.C.: American Enterprise Institute, 1979.

———. *The Oil Transfer Problem and International Economic Stability*. Princeton Essays in International Finance, no. 113. Princeton, N.J.: International Finance Section, Princeton University, 1975.

———, and Forte, Francesco. "Interest-Rate Policy and External Balance." *Quarterly Journal of Economics* 83 (May 1969): 242–62.

———, and Laney, Leroy. "Monetarism, Budget Deficits, and Wage Push Inflation: The Cases of Italy and the United Kingdom." Banca Nazionale del Lavoro *Quarterly Review* (December 1978): 315–31.

———, and Mullen, John. "The Effects of Alternative International Monetary Systems on Macro-Economic Discipline and the Political Business Cycle."

Claremont Economic Papers. Claremont, Calif.: Claremont Graduate School, 1980.

Williamson, John. "Exchange Rate Flexibility and Reserve Use." *Scandinavian Journal of Economics* 78 (1976): 327–39.

————. "International Liquidity: A Survey." *Economic Journal* 83 (September 1973): 685–764.

————. "Techniques to Control International Reserves: Comment." In *The New International Monetary System*, edited by Robert Mundell and Jacques J. Polak. New York: Columbia University Press, 1977.

————. *The Failure of World Monetary Reform, 1971–74*. New York: New York University Press, 1977.

Willms, Manfred. "Money Creation in the Eurocurrency Market." *Weltwirtschaftliches Archiv*, Heft 2 (1976): 201–30.

Witteveen, H. Johannes. "A Conversation with Mr. Witteveen." *Finance and Development* (September 1978): 6–9.

————. "On the Control of International Liquidity." *IMF Survey* 4 (October 28, 1975): 313–16.

Yeager, Leland B. *International Monetary Relations*. New York: Harper and Row, 1976.

SELECTED AEI PUBLICATIONS

The AEI Economist, Herbert Stein, ed., published monthly (one year, $10; single copy, $1)

Housing: Federal Policies and Programs, John C. Weicher (161 pp., $6.25)

The Limitations of General Theories in Macroeconomics, T.W. Hutchison (31 pp., $3.25)

Unemployment Benefits: Should There Be a Compulsory Federal Standard? Joseph M. Becker (63 pp., $4.25)

The Economy: Can We Avert Disaster? John Charles Daly, mod. (33 pp., $3.75)

Deterring Criminals: Policy Making and the American Political Tradition, Jeffrey Leigh Sedgwick (50 pp., $4.25)

The Economics of the Davis-Bacon Act: An Analysis of Prevailing-Wage Laws, John P. Gould and George Bittlingmayer (89 pp., $4.25)

Conglomerate Mergers: Causes, Consequences, and Remedies, George J. Benston (76 pp., $4.25)

Amtrak: The National Railroad Passenger Corporation, George W. Hilton (80 pp., $4.25)

Prices subject to change without notice.

AEI ASSOCIATES PROGRAM

The American Enterprise Institute invites your participation in the competition of ideas through its AEI Associates Program. This program has two objectives:

The first is to broaden the distribution of AEI studies, conferences, forums, and reviews, and thereby to extend public familiarity with the issues. AEI Associates receive regular information on AEI research and programs, and they can order publications and cassettes at a savings.

The second objective is to increase the research activity of the American Enterprise Institute and the dissemination of its published materials to policy makers, the academic community, journalists, and others who help shape public attitudes. Your contribution, which in most cases is partly tax deductible, will help ensure that decision makers have the benefit of scholarly research on the practical options to be considered before programs are formulated. The issues studied by AEI include:

- Defense Policy
- Economic Policy
- Energy Policy
- Foreign Policy
- Government Regulation
- Health Policy
- Legal Policy
- Political and Social Processes
- Social Security and Retirement Policy
- Tax Policy

For more information, write to:

AMERICAN ENTERPRISE INSTITUTE
1150 Seventeenth Street, N.W.
Washington, D.C. 20036